Perfect Love: The Path to Glory

Perfect Love: The Path to Glory

The eternal beauty of growing in the love of God—and how to be an instrument of love in a decaying generation

And we have known and believed the love that God has for us. God is love, and he who abides in love abides in God, and God in Him. — 1 John 4:16

Grace Ozioma Onotu

Perfect Love
Published by
Inscript Publishing
a division of Dove Christian Publishers
P.O. Box 611
Bladensburg, MD 20710-0611
www.inscriptpublishing.com

Copyright © 2018 by Grace Ozioma Onotu

Cover Design by Raenita Wiggins

All rights reserved. No part of this publication may be used or reproduced without permission of the publisher, except for brief quotes for scholarly use, reviews or articles.

Scripture citations marked NIV are from the the Holy Bible, New International Version®, NIV® Copyright © 1973, 1978, 1984, 2011 by Biblica, Inc.® Used by permission. All rights reserved worldwide.

Library of Congress Control Number: to be added

ISBN: 9781732112506

Printed in the United States of America

Dedication

This work is dedicated to God Almighty, who has loved me with an everlasting love.

Acknowledgments

I thank God for His faithfulness and love towards me. Words alone cannot express my eternal gratitude for His marvellous help along my life journey. He is my everything, and the reason I live.

To my parents, Mr and Mrs Onotu Ahmed and my siblings, I say thank you for your love and support. May the love of God never depart from our home. In Jesus's name, Amen.

Thanks to the men and women of God whom God has used as they shared their teachings, materials, and guidance to build me up and make me eternally focused and driven. I am especially and eternally grateful to Papa—Bishop David Oyedepo—for getting me rooted in God's incorruptible, infallible, and profitable word. To Bishop David Abioye: I thank you for your prayers and encouragement, sir! Thanks to Barrister Emeka Nwankpa for helping me to become a true intercessor. I appreciate your timely words, prayers, and encouragement. To Rev Sam Adeyemi, I say thank you for leading me to Christ through the exposition of the love of God.

To my spiritual mentors, Dr Paul Enenche and his wife, Dr Becky Enenche, I am eternally grateful for your prayers, show of love, encouragement, and timely words. To Dr Ezekiel Oyemomi, I say thank you for your consistency and unconditional love. To Uncle Ojukwu, Gen Salihu Ibrahim (Rtd), and Rev Aka, I thank you for being there always.

To my professional and life mentors, Professor A.

O. Malomo, Dr. Babajide Coker, Pastor Okechukwu Emmanuel Okechukwu, Dr Steve Ogan, and Dr Emmanuel Sokpo, I say thank you for every word of encouragement, direction, and belief in me.

I extend my appreciation to Barrister Grace Ovba, Mr Olushola Obaisi, Mrs Blessing Okoh, Itode Igweke, Mrs Ozigi, Mrs Chioma Okafor, Ms Dooshyma Kumbur, Mr Dele Adebayo, and Mrs Uche Areghan for their encouragement and faith in me.

Contents

Dedication	v
Acknowledgments	vi
Preface	xi
Introduction	xvi
Chapter One	1
The Triumphant Life of Living and Walking in God's Love	1
Chapter Two	13
Biblical Perspective of Love	13
What Biblical Love Is	15
The Things We Are Commanded Not to Love	20
Appreciating God's Love	22
Chapter Three	25
The Foundation of Loving God	25
What Loving God Does for Us:	45
What Loving Others Will Do for Us:	45
What Loving Others Will Do for Them:	46
Chapter Four	47
Growing in the Love of God	47
How Do I Grow in the Love of God?	48
Why It Seems Difficult for People to Grow in God's Love	61
Chapter Five	65
Experiencing the Reality of God's Love Daily	65
God's Love: The Road to a Happy and Fulfilling Life	67
Love: The Formula for Winning Spiritual Warfare	71
God's Love: A Canopy of Protection	73
Love: The Pathway to Internal Freedom and Magnanimity	75
God's Love: A Pathway to Accelerated Spiritual Growth	80
Walking in God's Love is to Daily Walk in His Wisdom	81
Love: The Road to Unity and Success	81
Love: Eternity on Course and Eternity Secured	83
Implications of a Closed Heart	85
How Do We Bring God's Love Into Our Relationships?	87
Chapter Six	89
Manifesting God's Love in Our Relationships	89
Working Out Godly Relationships in Our Families	93
Working Out Godly Relationships With Unbelievers	96
Working Out Godly Relationships in Friendship	98

Homosexuality/Lesbianism ... 107
Chapter Seven ... **111**
Saving the World with God's Love ... 111
What Is the Tabernacle of David All About? ... 112
How Do We Go About It? ... 114
Chapter Eight ... **131**
End Time Warning: Our Love Must Not Go Cold! ... 131
Jesus Is Coming Soon! Maranatha! ... 135
Epilogue ... **137**
Other Books by
Dr. Grace Ozioma Onotu ... **138**

Preface

This book is born out of a heart burdened by seeing the church of Jesus Christ in a state of mediocrity and mundaneness. Yet, I am hopeful that it will rise to its highest call of loving God and humankind. Love, being the driving force into eternity, must be given its urgent attention and its due place in our teaching in this end time. It will help us get ready for the return of our bridegroom: Jesus Christ. As the potential spotless bride of Christ, the church cannot afford to have a superficial relationship with God and His creation. Superficiality does not make us real and authentic; it cannot bring us into the fullness of our call as God's royal priesthood and a holy nation.

To fulfill our call as His kings and priests here on earth and to consummate our relationship with Him in the marriage supper of the Lamb, we must develop a deep love relationship with God as the work of His hands. Love flows from us to His creation by fulfilling His purpose for creation. If we do not understand God's eternal love for us, we will not be able to respond to Him—or have enough faith in Him who is invisible yet active in our lives.

As I watch people go about their activities within and outside the church environment, I see a whole lot of differences between their attitudes as part of these two settings. People come to church raising holy hands, looking pious, and blessing the name of the Lord; however, in their homes, their respective businesses, and society at large, their utterances, relationships with others, and decisions made in their places of service and authority do not reflect the values of Jesus Christ.

So much disunity among believers and church leaders exist that one wonders what went wrong or what happened to the legacy and words of our Lord Jesus Christ. We hear of atrocities and abominations among Christians. One wonders if such things should be named among us, which I believe should be a concern to anyone that genuinely loves the Lord. However, the people of the world are watching us; we are to be the salt of the earth and the light of the world (Matthew 5:13-14). Where did we get it all wrong? What happened along the way? What can we do to arrest the schisms, the indifference to one another, and the unrighteous acts in the church in order to affect the world positively for the Lord? As children of God, we are pilgrims here on earth, as David rightly said (Psalm 119:19-20). Though we are in the world, we are not of this world. We have a destination, and that is to spend eternity with the Lord. Sometimes, I think we read the Bible convincing ourselves that we believe all that is written there; however, in reality, our hearts are full of doubts. That is why it is so easy to behave like people of the world.

We are pilgrims here on earth to change the world for good so that Christ will come to us and return us to our homeland: a place prepared for us by our Lord Jesus Christ. How do we retrace our steps to the very foundation of our faith, which is the love that God has for humankind that made Him give His only begotten Son to save us and reconcile us to Himself? We have been so carried away by what to eat and drink, which house to live in, and building empires for ourselves that we have forgotten God's commandments.

It is not possible to serve at God's altar as His priests without love for Him and His creation. Our ministrations to Him as His priests must be born out of love. As we stand before Him on behalf of our nation, community, friends, and loved ones, we need love in our hearts to intercede without a judgmental attitude. As kings who will reign here on earth, we need His love in our hearts to rule in alignment with His will and to serve our generation in the fear of the Lord like David, as testified to in Acts 13:36:

For David, after he had served his own generation by the will of God, fell asleep, was buried with his fathers, and saw corruption.

How David was able to serve his generation in the will of God is found in 2 Samuel 23:2-3:

"The Spirit of the LORD spoke by me, and His word was on my tongue. The God of Israel said, The Rock of Israel spoke to me, 'He who rules over men must be just, ruling in the fear of God." These were his last words before he died. This is what one of my mentors, Dr Steve Ogan, calls "righteous rulership through divine relationship."

No wonder God says in Acts 15:16-17:

"After this I will return and will rebuild the tabernacle of David, which has fallen down; I will rebuild its ruins, and I will set it up; so that the rest of mankind may seek the LORD,

even all the Gentiles who are called by My name, says the LORD *who does all these things."*

Without love, we cannot serve in the fear of the Lord, because power corrupts. Therefore, love is the only virtue that can put authority under God's jurisdiction without anarchy or abuse of power. We will talk more about this in the following chapters.

The core message of this book is that only the love of God can make us reign triumphantly here on earth and prepare us for eternity. Further, only the love of God can grant us internal freedom, destroy lust, and help us to walk with integrity and purity of heart; thereby preparing us daily to become the spotless bride of Christ, worthy and qualified to be united with Him in eternal marriage.

Only love can take us to that place of heavenly mindedness and eternity consciousness, as we wait for the return of our bridegroom who will qualify us to be partakers of the New Jerusalem, where according to Revelation 22:3-5:

"And there shall be no more curse, but the throne of God and of the Lamb shall be in it, and His servants shall serve Him. They shall see His face, and His name shall be on their foreheads. There shall be no light there: they need no lamp nor light of the sun, for the Lord God gives them light. And they shall reign forever and ever." Praise God! Amen.

I sincerely believe that God is calling His people back to the biblical concept of love in order to conquer the world in these last days; that the message of the kingdom will reach all the nations of the earth in preparation for the return of our King Jesus Christ. This message will also help us to find solutions to the majority of the problems on earth. Only love can heal the nations of the earth. It is the only thing that cannot fail, because where love is, God is.

Introduction

This book expounds on the love of God and the capacity of every believer and follower of Jesus Christ to love as He loves by being an epitome of love to a decaying society. It also relates how the love of God should reflect in our relationships with God and our fellow human beings—and how to grow in the love of God.

It encourages us about the need to endure to the end in following the Lord and obeying His commandments. There is a reward for enduring to the end, according to the book of Revelation.

Perfect Love: The Path to Glory, I believe, will impart us afresh with the Spirit of love to overcome all that is not of God in our lives and society. It will help us to see that our very end is to be like God. If that is the goal, then we must become what the Bible says: that God is love.

If we heed the biblical concept of love, the Holy Spirit will always be there to impart it to us and also enable us to be kingdom love practitioners.

God bless you.

Chapter One

The Triumphant Life of Living and Walking in God's Love

The subject of love has been a vital issue for a long time especially in the twenty-first century. Many words have been spoken and written about it; yet, the world grows colder without love. We experience heartlessness, brutality, murder, heartbreak, and war everywhere. Even in the Christian fold, we do not see much difference. We see churches rise against one another, and brothers and sisters lying to and cheating one another. The church is meant to be the epitome of love—a living example to people in the world. This has led to confusion and worldly principles about this subject in the church.

Jesus said we are not of this world even though we live in this world (John 17:14-16). This is a very serious message to us as people of God. In everything we do and wherever we find ourselves, we need not forget Jesus's statement. We are the regenerated ones, born of the Spirit of God. We are the ambassadors of heaven. The immortal Spirit of the Living God dwells in us. The people of the world are not regenerated in the Spirit, and so, have no capacity for the things that are of God. Because of this, nothing that comes from the world gives life.

In the body of Christ today, so many things are going wrong. Teenagers and adolescents are lost to drugs, sexual lusts, perversions, and ungodly relationships. They also experience ungodly interactions on the phone, internet, and television. Families experience divorce and lack a heart for God. In Europe and other parts of the world, churches have turned into monuments and tourism sites. The hearts of the people have departed from God.

The devil has subtly crept in to displace our first love: Jesus. He gives us the power to love and live as He did when He walked on the earth. The devil knows the power and influence we will have if we give to the Lord much of the time we spend on all electronic devices and ungodly relationships. That is why he, the devil, would hardly sit and watch people serve God without misleading them.

Many are going down the road of hellfire all in the name of civilisation and what some call modern Christianity. There is no such thing as modern Christianity; instead, but a refusal to detach ourselves from the ways of the world, so we bring them along with us to the church.

As disciples of Jesus Christ, we are His ambassadors among foreign people and should not partake of their culture and forsake or amend heavenly principles to suit us. We are pilgrims here on earth; we are heavenly dwellers, and our end is to be with the Lord. For this reason, we are to attune our minds with the mind of Christ by renewing our minds daily as we study His lifestyle from His word. In doing so, we can begin to think and act like Him. Our definition and practice of love must be scripturally based — not based on the views of people of the world. Therefore, we should not refuse to take advantage of the regenerated Spirit in us to grow in love and be like Jesus.

Chapter One

Irrespective of where we were born, come from, or what our past has been, the scriptures cannot be changed to suit us, because God's standard is not the same as the world's. Bringing the world's concept of love into the kingdom of God will never profit us or make us Christlike.

Jesus Christ is the epitome of love. While He walked on earth, He was love personified. This helped Him fulfill His mission of healing, deliverance, and generosity with no scandal or atrocity in all His relationships with both males and females. He triumphed over temptations and brought reconciliation between God and humankind on the Cross of Calvary. He expects this to be our testimony: to triumph over sin and the wickedness in the world. He knew no sin but was made sinful for us because of His love for us.

Colossians 2:6–15 gives us a picture of what Jesus did for us on the Cross of Calvary. Read with me: *"As you therefore have received Christ Jesus the Lord, so walk in Him, rooted and built up in Him and established in the faith, as you have been taught abounding in it with thanksgiving. Beware lest anyone cheat you through philosophy and empty deceit, according to the tradition of men, according to the basic principles of the world and not according to Christ. For in Him dwells all the fullness of the Godhead bodily: and you are complete in Him, who is the head of all principality and power. In Him you were also circumcised with the circumcision made without hands, by putting off the body of the sins of the flesh, by the circumcision of Christ, buried with Him in baptism, in which you also were raised with Him through faith in the working of God, who raised Him from the dead. And you being dead in your trespasses and the uncircumcised of your flesh, He has made alive together with Him, having forgiving you all trespasses, having wiped out the handwriting of requirements that was against us, which was contrary to us. And He has taken it out of the way, having nailed it to the cross. Having disarmed principalities and powers, He made a public spectacle of them, triumphing over them in it."*

From the above scriptures, we see that if we are not built and rooted in Christ, it will be easy to be manipulated in the world, to be tossed around by the traditions of humankind and be enslaved. If we do not know the truth of what is freely ours, we will walk in darkness and will never live a victorious and glorious life. We have been raised with Christ from terrestrial to celestial, and that is the place of love, where God dwells; a place of no sin, no sorrow, because Christ has nailed every contrary handwriting of requirements against us to the cross—every sin, sickness, poverty, and condemnation has been judged. We may ask, "If Christ has done all these things for us, why are we still living defeated and broken lives? Why does so much hatred and fear of the future exist? Why do church people still commit suicide?"

I believe that our hearts have departed from the Lord—our first love. Even when we claim to have surrendered all to Him, many things—such as materialism, career, marriage, money, titles, and position—still contend with the love of God in our hearts. This was the case with the Israelites; God became angry with them. In our generation too, things are deteriorating so fast that one begins to understand why Jesus asked a vital question in Luke 18:8b, *"Nevertheless, when the Son of Man comes, will He really find faith on the earth?"*

Jeremiah 2:11–19 says,

"Has a nation changed its gods, which are not gods? But My people have changed their Glory, for what does not profit. Be astonished, O heavens, at this, and be horribly afraid; be very desolate" says the Lord. *"For My people have committed two evils: they have forsaken Me, the fountain of living waters, and hewn themselves cisterns broken cisterns – that can hold no water. Is Israel a servant? Is he a homeborn slave? Why is he plundered? The*

Chapter One

young lion roared at him, and growled; they made his land waste; His cities are burn without inhabitant. Also the people of Noph and Tahpanhes have broken the crown of your head. Have you not brought this on yourself, in that you have forsaken the LORD your God, when He led you in the way? And now why take the road to Egypt, to drink the waters of Sihor? Or why take the road to Assyria, to drink the waters of the River? Your own wickedness will correct you, and your backslidings will rebuke you. Know therefore and see that it is an evil and bitter thing, that you have forsaken the LORD your God and the fear of Me is not in you," says the Lord GOD of hosts.

When our hearts depart from the Lord, we become empty. We search for satisfaction where there is none. We do things that attract curses and problems in our lives. Without God, life is full of crisis, hopelessness, and desolation. We begin to scheme for love in the wrong places, yet the place of God cannot be replaced by any other. This is why Jeremiah 2:33 asks, *"Why do you beautify your way to seek love? Therefore you have also taught the wicked women your ways."* The New Living Translation puts it this way: *"How you plot and scheme to win your lovers. The most experienced prostitute could learn from you!"*

You will agree with me that this is the state of Christ's church today. I am sure someone is wondering what I mean by this. The truth is that many of us proclaim our love for God, yet we would not cross certain boundaries for Him. If it is our earthly sensual relationships, we could do anything to keep a husband from running away. We could go the extra mile to ensure success in our careers, but when it comes to God, we say that God understands. Everything we desire—including that husband or lover we want to keep by all means—and every other thing that is competing with the love of God in our hearts, can indeed be achieved if we understand that it is only in the love of God that we can achieve them without sweat, if we would abide in God's love. No matter what we do to beautify our ways in searching for love, there is no truer or greater love anywhere outside God.

Men and women who do not love God cannot genuinely love themselves; in turn, that makes it difficult for them to love others. What do I mean by this? If people love God, they will understand the principles of God guiding their lives, and they will adhere to them. In adhering to God's principles, they find a purpose and how to fulfill it. In doing that he makes his life fulfilling, which is the ultimate of self-love. But people who do not love God do not abide by His commandments. They do things that they think are right and pleasurable, yet they are detrimental to his life. This is why the Bible says, *"There is a road that seems right to a man, but the end leads to destruction"* (Proverbs 14:12).

We are a people appointed for God's praise to show forth His glory, as we read in Jeremiah 2:21: *"Yet I had planted you a noble vine, a seed of highest quality. How then have you turned before Me into the degenerate plant of an alien vine?"* God is asking us this question today. How does God feel when He sees us pervert His original intention for creation? That the people He created to have dominion over all things now subject themselves to behaviour such as lying, armed robbery, disobedience to parents and authorities, bestiality, homosexuality, and cheating? God has feelings, and it hurts Him when we disobey Him and do things wickedly. I do not know what the state of your heart is. But what I do know is that as individuals, we know how far we have departed from God or are distracted from His love. Let us examine our hearts in order to return to the Lord. The Lord desires an intimate love relationship with us; this will spur us to absolute obedience and dependence on Him. He is a great Lover to have, and only in Him can we have a triumphant life full of joy indescribable. God calls on every one of us today as He speaks from Jeremiah 4:1-2:

"If you will return, O Israel," says the Lord, *"Return to Me; and if you will put away your abominations out of My sight, then you shall not be moved. And you shall swear, 'the* Lord *lives,' in truth, in judgment, and in righteousness; The nations shall bless themselves in Him, and in Him they shall glory."* That is a call to our place of glory in life. It is a call to return to the Lord with all our hearts, and we shall never be moved. What a triumphant life we are called into!

The road of love is a path less travelled because not many people love to take this path to glory; it involves a lot. But it is a call to spiritual growth and maturity to those whose spirits are synced with God to birth his purpose on earth. These people are absolutely abandoned and yielded to Him; their lives are no longer theirs but possessed by the Spirit of God. They let go in the hand of faith, trusting God every step of the way that He will lead them through this world into eternity as they act as His instrument of love.

What is a triumphant life? Living and walking in God's love is a life that will reign here on earth transcending eternity, a life that will be among the saints spoken of in Revelation 21:2-5. *"Then I, John, saw the holy city, New Jerusalem, coming down out of heaven from God, prepared as a bride adorned for her husband. And I heard a loud voice from heaven saying, "Behold, the tabernacle of God is with men, and He will dwell with them, and they shall be His people, God Himself will be with them and be their God. And God will wipe away every tear from their eyes; there shall be no more death, nor sorrow, nor crying. There shall be no more pain, for the former things have passed away." Then He who sat on the throne said, "Behold, I make all things new." And He said to me "Write, for these words are true and faithful."*

How Can the Love of God Make Us Triumphant in Daily Living?

We can live triumphant daily in the love of God by being conscious of Who God is—His sovereignty, and eternal nature and the eternal life He has given to those who believe in Him. The Bible says that God has poured His love into our hearts through His Spirit (Romans 5:5). Ecclesiastes 3:11 says that God has put eternity in our hearts.

He put eternity in our hearts and shed His love abroad in our hearts so that love will guard us through our daily living eternally. What is eternal life? It is the life of God at work in the life of a believer. It is also called the Zoe kind of life; this is what enables us to live a godly life here. If He has already put eternity in our hearts, we are to be living the kind of life that exists from eternity to eternity—as God does. Oh my God! We are not to wait till we die before we start living a godly life. A heavenly lifestyle is meant to be our lifestyle here in the world. We are heavenly dwellers, the Bible says. We are seated with Christ in heavenly places far above principalities and power. Beloved, this is who we are. This is the life we are to be conscious of daily to be victorious on earth as believers. No wonder the Bible says that we are to be perfected in love so that we may have boldness on the Day of Judgment. Because as He is, so are we in this world (1 John 4:17). If we are as Christ is in this world, then we are entitled and should live the kind of exemplary life that He lived while on earth.

In Ephesians 3:14-19, Paul the apostle wrote to the Ephesian Church, praying to God on their behalf. Read with me in The Living Bible:

Chapter One

"When I think of the wisdom and scope of his plan, I fall down on my knees and pray to the Father of all the great family of God — some of them already in heaven and some down here on earth — that out of his glorious, unlimited resources he will give you the mighty inner strengthening of his Holy Spirit. And I pray that Christ will be more and more at home in your hearts, living within you as you trust in him. May your roots go down deep into the soil of God's marvelous love; and may you be able to feel and understand, as all God's children should, how long, how wide, how deep, and how high his love really is; and to experience this love for yourselves, though it is so great that you will never see the end of it or fully know or understand it. And so at last you will be filled up with God himself.

From the above scriptures, we read the prayer of the Spirit of God through the apostle Paul to the church. We see that the most important factor that enables us to operate in the fullness of God is our ability to comprehend and live in the love that Jesus Christ has for us. This will be impossible without us. As individuals, being rooted and grounded in love. In Ephesians 3:16, Paul the apostle wanted all people to have the power to understand how deep the love of God is. This is why he prayed that the Spirit of God would strengthen them in their inner selves. It is only by the Holy Spirit that our hearts can be enlightened and rooted in the great love of God. When we can comprehend and come to terms with the depth of God's love, to accept it and to live in it, then we can be filled with the fullness of God. To be filled with the fullness of God is our ultimate desire as His children; from this scripture, the prescription for attaining the reality of this desire is in our ability to comprehend, live, and walk in this divine love.

The Bible says in Colossians 1:19, *"For it pleased the Father that in Him all the fullness should dwell."* This was expounded upon in Colossians 2:9–10: *"For in Him dwells all the fullness of the Godhead bodily: and you are complete in Him, who is the head of all principality and power."*

If all the fullness of the Godhead dwells in Christ bodily, that means everything in God and the Holy Spirit dwells in Him bodily. The same Christ described in Hebrews 1:3: *"the brightness of His glory and the express image of His person, upholding all things by the word of His power."* Then we see the in-depth implication of being rooted in the love of God because the scriptures cannot be broken. If we abide in love, we abide in God—and God in us. There is no way anyone would have a deep understanding of this and settle for a lesser life. A life lived and walked in love is a triumphant life—far above principalities and powers. If Jesus Christ is the head of all principalities and powers and we are complete in Him, we understand that love is a powerful force of the Spirit. The devil cannot stand where there is an outpouring of love.

Brothers and sisters, I enjoin that we read this book with an open heart and receive the message as an open letter from heaven to enter into our rest and place in God.

The devil fights the hearts and minds of people every day, deluding them that no one loves them, thereby making them do all manner of things against God and their fellow humans. If only we knew, not just in our knowing but having the power to grasp and understand God's love towards us, then we will do anything to live in it and not believe the lies of the devil.

Some time ago, a young cousin of mine who stayed with us suddenly began to behave in an unusual manner in school. My siblings became worried about her change in attitude; they were scared she might become wayward. Initially, I kept my peace and did not want to involve myself,

Chapter One

having considered that the intervention of my mum, dad, and younger sister had not been able to achieve much. The situation got worse, and everyone seemed to leave her to herself. I became worried because I suggested that she stay with my parents—and I brought her there. My mum wanted her out of the house because she felt she did not comply with her rules and regulations.

All hope seemed lost, as everyone—except one of my younger brothers—no longer cared about what she did, since they did not see or expect any visible positive change. One day, the Holy Spirit ministered to me: *Do not watch the enemy snatch her destiny away.* At that point, I knew I had a task; it hit me that God did not, by chance, use me to bring her to the house; He had a purpose for me in her life. An older friend of mine advised me not to be aggrieved towards her as the others were. My friend encouraged me to use wisdom and the love of God. I gradually interacted with her as if I were not aware of how badly she was behaving, or how careless she had become. I grew closer to her; I began calling her more often than I had been, and I sent her text messages. I told her how much I love her and how much God loves her as well. The more I did this, the more open she became towards me. I prayed with her, counselled her, and interceded for God's intervention.

Within a short period, I spoke with my parents and siblings. By God's grace, I was able to convince them that things were not as they thought. The confusion intended by the devil was squashed by God. She returned to the house a totally different person, in spite of her mistakes. Unknown to me—and while all this was happening—she had given her life to Jesus Christ, a conversion from Islam. The enemy was not happy about it and was attempting to undermine her new faith. At the end of the day, she was not just welcomed into the house, but was accepted with her new faith as a Christian until she moved out of our house. This was a hard task because all my family members are still Muslims. I was the only Christian in the family before her conversion. Two days after this victory, the Lord showed me that the enemy was after the girl's place in the kingdom of God.

My cousin later told me she behaved that way because she thought no one loved and cared about her anymore. My people thought she was rude and unbearable. The enemy created an unnecessary contention by planting his evil seeds of thought in her mind; however, the love of God that is above every principality dethroned those thoughts and brought them into the obedience of Christ.

I do not know what your situation is like. I do not know whose love has failed or is failing you, but there is a love that does not fail; there is a love that does not abandon; there is a love that is eternal, glorious, and powerful. It is the love of God. If you feel that no one loves you, be foolish enough to believe that the invisible, all-powerful, and all-wise God loves you with an everlasting love, and that you are the apple of His eye (Deuteronomy 32:10; Zechariah 2:8). If only you will believe these words, your life will be radically changed. You will be delivered from the lies of the enemy.

Chapter Two

Biblical Perspective of Love

The Bible is a book filled with love stories. The greatest love story ever told is found in the Bible, and that is the story of the most powerful King of heaven and earth — Almighty God, creator of all on earth and in heaven and who became man to redeem humanity back to Himself. The word of God became flesh to dwell among us (John 1:14) — to teach us how to live, to show us the path of life, and impart His very life to us. In the end, He died for our sins and was raised for our justification.

The gospel of Jesus Christ is a gospel of love; this love is all-encompassing and cannot be defined by human words. The Bible, which has the final authority, already tells us that God is love. We can clearly understand why God is merciful, gracious, kind, humble, giving, and compassionate. Jesus made us understand the importance of this great virtue when one of the Pharisees asked him which was the greatest among the commandments. Jesus said in Matthew 22:37–40: *"You shall love the LORD your God with all your heart, with all your soul, and with all your mind. This is the first and the great commandment. And the second is like it: you shall love your neighbour as yourself. On these two commandments hang all the Law and the Prophets."*

From the above scriptures, we see that love is the greatest thing in the kingdom of God. To buttress this point further, let us look at 1 Corinthians 13:13: *"And now abide faith, hope, love, these three; but the greatest of these is love."* We need no third witness in the scripture to let this sink into us that this is the greatest virtue ever. Already, the apostle Paul in 1 Corinthians chapter 13 had compared love to other great things we talk about in the kingdom, such as faith that moves mountains, prophecies, knowing mysteries, and good works. We see the weakness of these forces of the spirit without love; he proved love as the only thing that cannot fail. I sincerely believe that faith and hope are a means to an end, and that end is love. We need faith and hope here so that someday we will see the Lord and be with Him, while love is dwelling in us to become like Him — to be worthy, to be consummated with Him at the marriage supper of the Lamb. At that point, faith and hope will be done away with, while love will be consummated. Alleluia!

We realise from the scriptures that the natural human being has no capacity to love because love is life, and the only source of life is God; so, only the regenerated person born of the Spirit of God has the capacity to love. The Bible says in 1 John 3:14-15: *"We know that we have passed from death to life, because we love the brethren. He who does not love his brother abides in death. Whoever hates his brother is a murderer, and you know that no murderer has eternal life abiding in him."* I am sure you are wondering why these verses emphasize loving the brethren in relation to life and death and not the love for God. The Bible makes us understand that the real test of our love for God is our love for our fellow human beings created in the image of God that we see. Read 1 John 4:20-21: *"If someone says, 'I love God' and hates his brother, he is a liar; for he who does not love his brother whom he has seen, how can he love God whom he has not seen?" And this commandment we have from Him: that he who loves God must love his brother also."*

What Biblical Love Is

1. It is a commandment.

It is necessary for every believer to love God and his neighbours — whether they are believers or not — as we have seen in Matthew 22:37-40.

2. Love is not a feeling but a Spirit, because God is love.

1 John 4:16: *"And we have known and believed the love that God has for us. God is love, and he who abides in love abides in God and God in him."* The Bible also tells us that "God has not given us a spirit of fear, but of power, of love, and of a sound mind" (2 Timothy 1:7).

3. Love is a personality, and that personality is the Holy Spirit of God.

Colossians 3:14 enjoins us, *"But above all these things put on love, which is the bond of perfection."* Romans 13:14 says, *"But put on the Lord Jesus Christ, and make no provision for the flesh, to fulfill its lust."*

4. Love is not lustful because it is holy.

God is holy. From the scripture above, we see that we cannot put on Christ and be lustful, which is why it is the bond of perfection; only God is perfect. I love the way Watchman Nee puts it in his book *The Spiritual Man, Volume 2*. He said, "However nothing is more important in a believer's consecration than his love. Whether his consecration is true or false depends upon whether or not there is consecration of love. Love is the touchstone of consecration."

5. Love is unconditional.

We did nothing to deserve the love of God. The Bible says: "We love Him because He first loved us" (1 John 4:19).

Note this reading: "...while we were still sinners, Christ died for us" (Romans 5:8). This is real love from a real God. This is the same unconditional love that God has poured in our hearts by His Holy Spirit. Then we can love to the same extent that Christ loved us to undertake our commission to win souls for the kingdom of God.

6. Love keeps us from sinning against God and against our fellow human beings.

Jesus said upon the first and second commandments hang all the Law and the Prophets (Matthew 22:40). Genuine love naturally stirs obedience. You would not want to hurt the one you love; this is why love is said to be the fulfillment of the law.

7. Love is to give us boldness on the Day of Judgment: because as He is, so are we in this world.

1 John 4:17: *"Love has been perfected among us in this: that we may have boldness in the day of judgment: because as He is, so are we in this world."*

I think we have allowed ourselves to miss so many things that we have been entrusted with. Our Lord has bestowed so much confidence and trust in us to reign on earth and dethrone Satan so that we will not be robbed of the eternal life He has given to us.

If we receive eternal life when we confess Him as Lord and saviour, but refuse to surrender our hearts absolutely to Him for His power to work in us, to perfect and make us as He is — to be conformed into His image of love — how will we be able to live this Zoe kind of life? How can we be as He is in this world? Will we really be bold to face Him on Judgment Day? We clearly see here that love is such a potent force. If we allow the Holy Spirit to impart it in our spirits and we grow in the knowledge of it, combined with proving our love to God by abiding in His love, obeying His commandments, and loving our neighbours in truth and in deed, then love becomes a lifestyle. The devil and his demons are disempowered from carrying out their machinations in our lives and society because they cannot stand the fire of God's love. This secures our eternal place in God till the end.

8. Love is light because God is light.

Wherever love is, truth reigns and triumphs — which is why love never fails. 1 John 1:5-7 says, *"This is the message which we have heard from Him and declare to you, that God is light and in Him is no darkness at all. If we say that we have fellowship with Him, and walk in darkness, we lie and do not practise the truth. But if we walk in the light as He is in the light, we have fellowship with one another, and the blood of Jesus His Son cleanses us from all sin."*

The NIV Women's Study Bible has this to say on love and the Christian life. The passage reads: "Love is the most striking evidence of whether or not someone is in Christ. The love we have for others provides the assurance that we have moved from the way of darkness and death to the way of life."

9. Love does not fear.

1 John 4:18 says, *"There is no fear in love; but perfect love casts out fear, because fear involves torment. But he who fears has not been made perfect in love."* As we read before, God has not given us a spirit of fear but a spirit of power, of love, and a sound mind. My brothers and sisters: when this spirit of love is operational in our lives, we will experience what it means to be free indeed in Christ Jesus. The Bible says, "whom the Son has set free is free indeed" (John 8:36); that freedom is wholly enjoyed in the love of God, which makes our life rich and magnanimous to walk in the newness of life eternal in Christ Jesus (Romans 6:4).

10. Love gives.

Love gave the greatest gift ever recorded in John 3:16: *"For God so loved the world that He gave His only begotten Son, that whoever believes in Him should not perish but have everlasting life."* Also, in 1 John 3:17-18, we read, *"But whoever has this world's goods, and sees his brother in need, and shuts up his heart from him, how does the love of God abide in him? My little children, let us not love in word or in tongue, but in deed and in truth."*

11. Love forgives.

When we love, we do not hold grudges in our hearts, and we are not easily offended. Some people are even offended in God. But the truth is that we do not love God because of what we can get from Him. He has already given us the greatest gift for which we cannot thank Him enough forever; it is unwise to be offended in God.

More so, with our fellow human beings, we should follow Jesus's example. In Matthew 18:21-22, Peter asked Him how often he should forgive a brother who sinned against him. Jesus said, *"I do not say, up to seven times, but up to seventy times seven."*

12. Love does not make others stumble.

Love makes us our brother's keeper and creates demands on us from the Lord, which is why Jesus said in Matthew 18:6, *"But whoever causes one of these little ones who believe in Me to sin, but it would be better for him if a millstone were hung around his neck, and he were drowned in the depth of the sea."* We now understand why 1 John 3:14 says, *"He who does not love his brother abides in death."* I sincerely believe that we are beginning to appreciate the fact that we do not have a sin problem, but we have a love problem. May the Lord give us understanding for others. In Jesus's name, amen.

13. Love is not judgmental.

Chapter Two

We read in John 8:4-11 the story of the woman caught in adultery who was brought to be stoned to death according to the law. The scribes and Pharisees were right; according to the law, she deserved to die. However, Jesus came into the world to show us how much He loves us and to teach us how he desires us to love one another. The very righteousness of God—birthed from eternity in God's everlasting love—and whose blood was shed as a token of love, was asked about how to punish an adulterer. Jesus knew the law. He knew she was to die; yet, His presence in the midst of humanity was to alter the dispensation of things. It would destroy hard-heartedness and hatred in us so that we would be able to hate sin and not the sinner; to judge sin and not the sinner with His love. Read with me: *"They said to Him, 'Teacher, this woman was caught in adultery, in the very act. Now Moses, in the law, commanded us that such should be stoned. But what do You say?' This they said, testing Him, that they might have something with which to accuse Him. But Jesus stooped down and wrote on the ground with His finger, as though He did not hear.*

So when they continued asking Him, He raised Himself up and said to them, 'He who is without sin among you, let him throw a stone first.' And again, He stooped down and wrote on the ground. Then those who heard it, being convicted by their conscience, went out one by one, beginning with the oldest even to the last. And Jesus was left alone, and the woman standing in the midst. When Jesus had raised Himself up and saw no one but the woman, He said to her, 'Woman, where are those accusers of yours? Has no one condemned you?' She said, 'No one, Lord.' And Jesus said to her, 'Neither do I condemn you; go and sin no more.'"

Jesus addressed the sin of the woman and the ones in the hearts of her accusers. Love saves by delivering the beloved from the very sin that seeks to destroy him or her. Jesus not only delivered the woman from her sin by His compassion and mercy, but also delivered the scribes and Pharisees from their judgmental way of life, which is a sinful lifestyle. That is what only love can do.

It is amazing how we are often so quick to judge one another. From the scriptures above we saw that it is only love that could rescue one from such obvious sin. The Bible says, *"…love will cover a multitude of sins* (1 Peter 4:8)." Jesus was not in support of the woman's act, but love overshadowed what *was* into *what could become* of her. This is the same way God rescued us from our sins. David the Psalmist said, *"Blessed is the man whom the Lord does not impute sin and his lawless deeds, He remembers no more* (Romans 4:7-8)." This is the blessedness of God's love; we can never fully know it until we make up our minds to work in it. This is what James 2:13 tells us, *"For judgment is without mercy to the one who has shown no mercy. Mercy triumphs over judgment."* We are all instruments of God's mercy and must in return be merciful by obeying the scriptural injunction that says, if anyone thinks he is spiritual, and finds another brother in error or sin, he should correct such a brother in love.

The Things We Are Commanded Not to Love

In 1 John 2:15-17, we are commanded as follows, *"Do not love the world or the things in the world. If anyone loves the world, the love of the Father is not in him. For all that is in the world, the lust of the flesh, the lust of the eyes, and the pride of life, is not of the Father but is of the world. And the world is passing away, and the lust of it; but he who does the will of God abides forever."*

The truth is, most of the problem we have in the church today is that, after leaving the world to come to Jesus, we find it difficult to detach from all that is in the world: the spoken language of the world, the friends and relationships we keep, the movies, and all manner of junk—such as pornography and other obscenities. No matter how hard we try, these things will choke the love of God and corrupt it in us; many people, especially youths, are still struggling with sin because of love of the world and the things in the world.

In 1 John 4:4-6 the Bible says, *"You are of God, little children, and have overcome them, because He who is in you is greater than he who is in the world. They are of the world. Therefore, they speak as of the world, and the world hears them. We are of God. He who knows God hears us; he who is not of God does not hear us. By this we know the spirit of truth and the spirit of error."*

Nothing in the world should compel our attention or make us think we are missing anything. If young people especially grasp that all this pleasure of the world takes us away from God, then we would be very careful and determined not to fall into the trap of the enemy.

The scripture we read above said the world is passing away and the lust that is in it but only those who do the will of the Father will abide. Let me ring a bell of warning, my beloved brothers and sisters: we are in the last days, and the scriptures have made us understand in Haggai 2:6-8 of the shakings that are to come upon the earth. The details of this shaking are revealed in Hebrews 12:26-29, *"...whose voice then shook the earth; but now He has promised, saying, 'Yet once more, I shake not only the earth, but also heaven.' Now this, 'Yet once more,' indicates the removal of those things that are being shaken, as of things that are made, that the things which cannot be shaken may remain. Therefore, since we are receiving a kingdom which cannot be shaken, let us have grace by which we may serve God acceptably with reverence and godly fear."*

These shakings are going to remove all that is not of God; this definitely includes people who live in disobedience, haters of God, and all the pleasures of the world. All that looks appealing in the world will be shaken—except that which is of God. That is why it is only those who do the will of God who will abide forever.

There is so much pleasure in God. But until we die totally to all that is in the world, we cannot take pleasure in the Lord. The ability to see clearly and appreciate this difference comes when we are fully ready to partake of the full joy of the Lord; to turn our eyes from the lies of the world to the truth of God and His word. The kingdom of God is unshakable because it is established on a sure foundation of truth, righteousness, and justice. Amen.

Appreciating God's Love

1. Accept it as real.
2. Love yourself as He loves you.
3. Open your heart for the Holy Spirit to shed the love of God in your heart.
4. Let every past hurt and bitterness go; otherwise, they will choke the love of God from your heart.
5. If you live in an abusive or unkind environment, do not let it affect the new love you are receiving in your heart.
6. Meditate on the wonders of the cross—of the pain, anguish, and suffering Jesus Christ endured to redeem you to God.
7. Allow your heart to daily grow in love by studying the life of Jesus Christ. He is love personified. Let the love of Jesus capture your heart and allow the Spirit of love to permeate your life—body, soul, and spirit.
8. Reach out to people in love; begin to display compassion, kindness, and forgiveness.
9. Be determined not to hurt God and others; you will

begin to experience the power of love to say no to sin because you cannot hurt the ones you love.

Perfect Love

Chapter Three

The Foundation of Loving God

"Jesus, I am resting, resting in the joy of what Thou art; I am finding out the greatness of Thy loving heart"
– Jean Sophia Pigott, 1876.

1. True Revelation of Whom God Is

The foundation on which men and women begin their Christian lives determines how far such people will work for and walk with the Lord. When a person comes to the saving knowledge of Jesus Christ based on the provision he will get from Him, the relationship will be shallow. This, our Lord Jesus Christ observed when He fed the multitude in John 6:25–27: *"And when they found Him on the other side of the sea, they said to Him, 'Rabbi, when did You come here?' Jesus answered them and said, 'Most assuredly, I say to you, you seek Me, not because you saw the signs, but because you ate of the loaves and were filled. Do not labour for the food which perishes, but for the food which endures to everlasting life, which the Son of Man will give you, because God the Father has set His seal on Him."* This is our situation in the church today. A lot of people come to God because they have specific needs, seeking bread and butter. And when they get it, they begin to relate to God as a business partner. When their needs are not met on time, they get frustrated, backslide, and become lukewarm in the church.

When people come to God on the foundation of Who He really is as the Creator of heaven and earth— who made humankind in His own image and likeness and gave them dominion over all things—who in spite of the betrayal in the garden of Eden, still loves them with everlasting love; only then will they see His power and love. Love made Him come down in the person of our Lord Jesus Christ to reconcile us back to Himself. It takes a person whose foundation is built on the revelation of Who God is to want to know Him more—let alone acknowledge and respond to His love. This is why God said in Jeremiah 4:22, *"For My people are foolish, they have not known Me. They are silly children, and they have no understanding. They are wise to do evil, but to do good, they have no knowledge."* There is something about having a revelation of God; it makes one seek to know Him more. It makes one run and chase after Him until one is able to catch Him. The power and will to love God is in the knowledge of Who He is.

Permit me to write about the awesome love of God. It was God's love for humankind that made Him create people in His own image. God created everything to make life comfortable for them before the Fall. You might ask me how I got that information. Read John 3:16 with me: *"For God so loved the world that He gave His only begotten Son, that whoever believes in Him should not perish but have everlasting life."* In spite of the betrayal by Adam and Eve in the garden of Eden, in spite of the disobedience of the children of Israel and their idolatry, God's love for humankind could not be quenched. Instead, He came down to demonstrate that love and to teach us how to live a pleasing and loving life. God's faithfulness has been from generation to generation. In spite of our unfaithfulness, God's nature has not changed; that nature is love.

The Bible says in Psalm 11:3: "When the foundations are destroyed, what can the righteous do?" There is a foundation on which people can encounter God that will birth an eternal love affair in their hearts. Jesus said in John 17:25-26 (NLT): *"O righteous Father, the world does not know you, but I do; and these disciples know you sent Me. And I have revealed you to them and will keep on revealing you. I will do this so that your love for Me may be in them and I in them."* No wonder that 1 John 5:20 says that the *"Son of God has come to give us understanding, that we might know the true God."* We also confirm this in Ephesians 3:1-4: *"For this reason I, Paul, the prisoner of Christ Jesus for you Gentiles – If indeed you have heard of the dispensation of the grace of God which was given to me for you, how that by revelation he made known to me the mystery (as I have briefly written already, by which, when you read, you may understand my knowledge in the mystery of Christ)."*

It is this knowledge that made the apostle Paul, who was once a hater of the faith, become an ardent lover of our Lord Jesus Christ. Paul loved God so much—to the point that he said in Philippians 1:21, *"For me, to live is Christ, and to die is gain."* These are not mere words, but words from a man who has a grasp on—and deep knowledge of—God. Hear him in Romans 8:35-39, *"Who shall separate us from the love of Christ? Shall tribulation, or distress, or persecution, or famine, or nakedness, or peril, or sword? As it is written: For your sake we are killed all day long; we are accounted as sheep for the slaughter. Yet in all these things we are more than conquerors through Him who loved us. For I am persuaded that neither death nor life, nor angels nor principalities nor powers, nor things present nor things to come, nor height nor depth, nor any other created thing, shall be able to separate us from the love of God which is in Christ Jesus our Lord."* I sincerely believe that the apostle Paul would not have survived all the persecutions he went through if not for the knowledge of God that birthed eternal purpose for God's kingdom in his heart.

In 1 John 1:1-3, we read what John said, *"That which was from the beginning, which we have heard, which we have seen with our eyes, which we have looked upon, and our hands have handled, concerning the Word of life – the life was manifested, and we have seen, and bear witness, and declare to you, that eternal life which was with the Father and was manifested to us – that which we have seen and heard we declare to you, that you also may have fellowship with us; and truly our fellowship is with the Father and His Son Jesus Christ."* That is a statement of confidence from a man who knows the God he serves and represents.

In Isaiah 6:5, the revelation of Who God is made Isaiah say: *"Woe is me, for I am undone! Because I am a man of unclean lips, and I dwell in the midst of a people of unclean lips; for my eyes have seen the King, the LORD of hosts."* No human being has ever encountered God in a genuine way and remained the same; that turning point always arrives where our hearts melt before the Lord. Desiring more of Him—as our hearts continually pant after Him (Psalm 42:1), an eternal affair is born between God and us.

When men and women have the revelation of Who God is—His attributes, character, and the nature of His love—they will leave everything to follow Him.

How Can God Be Revealed to Us?

From His Word and Scriptural Testimonies

The Bible makes us understand in John 1:1: *"In the beginning was the Word, and the Word was with God, and the Word was God."* When we spend time in His word and believe in all that is written, we know Him more. The more time we spend in the word of God, the more of God we know and become more like Him. In 2 Corinthians 3:18, the Bible says, *"But we all, with unveiled face, beholding as in a mirror the glory of the Lord, are being transformed into the same image from glory to glory, just as by the Spirit of the Lord."* We have to study and meditate on the word of God with the help of the Holy Spirit. The apostle Paul in Ephesians 1:17-18, prayed to God for His church: *"[T]hat the God of our Lord Jesus Christ, the Father of glory, may give to you the Spirit of wisdom and revelation in the knowledge of Him, the eyes of your understanding being enlightened; that you may know what is the hope of His calling, what are the riches of the glory of His inheritance in the saints."*

We need the revelation of God to be able to see Him as He really is, Until we see Him as He really is, we cannot comprehend the depth of His love for us. And until we are able to comprehend His love, we will never be able to respond to His love appropriately. This is the problem in the world and church today. Our love for God is the inheritance He has in us. Until we are captured and fascinated by Who God is, our hearts will not yearn for more of Him. Until we yearn for more of Him, we cannot tarry in His presence to worship and praise Him; and we cannot stand for His cause. His cause is for us to worship Him and to draw people to Him.

Our church services are filled with songs that appeal to our flesh and circumstances, but don't necessarily reverence and praise God in the beauty of His holiness. I believe we are beginning to see the difference between the believers of old and those of our generation. The believers of the Bible days— David, Daniel, Nehemiah, Esther, and others— were people who had a deep understanding of Who God is, upholding His testimonies from the time of old. Psalm 119:95-101 says, *"The wicked wait for me to destroy me, but I will consider Your testimonies. I have seen the consummation of all perfection, but Your commandment is exceedingly broad. Oh, how I love your law! It is my meditation all day. You, through Your commandments, make me wiser than my enemies; for they are ever with me. I have more understanding than all my teachers, for Your testimonies are my meditation. I understand more than the ancients, because I keep Your precepts. I have restrained my feet from every evil way, that I may keep Your word."* These are the words of David the Psalmist, whom the Lord testified of as *"a man after My own heart"* (Acts 13:22).

David loved the Lord; he grew in the knowledge of the Lord from His law and made a bold declaration: *"I have seen the consummation of all perfection."* This made David a triumphant king. God swore that his throne would be forever. No wonder our Lord Jesus Christ is from the lineage of David. Not only that, but even today, King David is still celebrated in Israel. God honours those who honour Him—even after they are no longer on the earth—by making them the joy of many generations.

We see a particular pattern in the lives of these saints of old because of their revelation of the knowledge of God. Let me briefly talk about Nehemiah and Daniel.

Nehemiah

In the land of captivity, Nehemiah served in the king's palace as his cupbearer. When he heard that the walls of Jerusalem were broken down and its gates burned with fire, he could have thanked God that he was not there to partake of the suffering. Instead, he became sorrowful. He wept and sought for what to do to ensure that Jerusalem was built. He fasted and prayed to God. In Nehemiah 1:1-11, we read: *"The words of Nehemiah, the son of Hachaliah. It came to pass in the month of Chislev, in the twentieth year, as I was in Shushan the citadel, that Hanani one of my brethren came with men from*

Judah; and I asked them concerning the Jews who had escaped, who had survived the captivity, and concerning Jerusalem. And they said to me, 'The survivors who are left from the captivity in the province are there in great distress and reproach. The walls of Jerusalem are also broken down, and its gates are burned with fire.' So it was when I heard these words that I sat down and wept, and mourned for many days: I was fasting and praying before the God of heaven.

"*And I said, 'I pray, L*ord *God of heaven, O great and awesome God, You who keep Your covenant and mercy with those who love You and observe Your commandments. Please, let Your ear be attentive and Your eyes open, that you may hear the prayer of Your servant which I pray before you now, day and night for the children of Israel Your servants, and confess the sins of the Children of Israel which we have sinned against You. Both my father's house and I have sinned. We have acted very corruptly against You, and have not kept the commandments, the statutes, nor the ordinances which You commanded Your servant Moses. Remember, I pray, the word that You commanded Your servant Moses, saying, "If you are unfaithful, I will scatter you amongst the nations; but if you return to Me, and keep My commandments and do them, though some of you were cast out to the farthest part of the heavens, yet I will gather them from there, and bring them to the place which I have chosen as a dwelling for My name." Now these are Your servants and Your people, whom you have redeemed by your great power, and by Your strong hand. O Lord, I pray, please let your ear be attentive to the prayer of Your servant, and to the prayer of Your servants who desire to fear Your name; and let Your servant prosper this day, I pray, grant him mercy in the sight of this man.'*

"*For I was the king's cupbearer."*

This is the story of a man who was enjoying time in the king's palace—living a life of safety, no fear, no anxiety, and possibly in luxury. But when he heard about the suffering of His brethren and the destruction of the city of the living God, his entire world seemed to come to an end. He completely forgot the life of the palace and instead associated with the suffering of his people. It was an emotional expression similar to what the Bible described in Hebrews 11:24-27: *"By faith Moses, when he became of age, refused to be called the son of Pharaoh's daughter, choosing rather to suffer affliction with the people of God than to enjoy the passing pleasures of sin, esteeming the reproach of Christ greater riches than the treasures in Egypt; for he looked to the reward. By faith he forsook Egypt, not fearing the wrath of the king; for he endured as seeing Him who is invisible."* This emotional expression reflects their understanding of whom they believe God to be from all they have heard or personally experienced of Him.

Nehemiah mourned and wept as one who was bereaved. He did not sit down to mourn continuously; he took steps of faith by first turning to God. He fasted and prayed. Nehemiah took the burden of an entire nation upon himself, repenting on their behalf before the Lord. It was an act of absolute faith and surrender to God. His willingness to do something about the situation made God grant his request. He first gave him favour before the king to allow him to embark on his journey to rebuild Jerusalem. Second, God made it possible for the king to render all the assistance he would require. Nehemiah risked his life for the love he had for God and his people. It takes a person with a solid foundation to stand up for a bigger cause. His knowledge of Whom God is propelled him to bear the burden of an entire nation and to take steps to ensure that Jerusalem was rebuilt. Nehemiah 1:10 states, *"Now these are Your servants and Your people, whom you have redeemed by Your great power, and by Your strong hand."* As I write this verse of the scriptures,

I am reminded of why God told Joshua in Joshua chapter 4 to raise a memorial to Him after they had crossed over the Jordan—which God had made a dry land so that they could tell their children in future of the wondrous acts of God, lest they forget. I sincerely believe that the testimonies of God's mighty work in Egypt and crossing over the Jordan gave Nehemiah the confidence that the God of his fathers is still alive and the same.

Today, how many of us are building memorials or binding God's testimonies of His wondrous acts in our lives for our children and grandchildren to see and ask questions? Instead, we delight in hiding our past and all we have been in Egypt before God delivered us by His mighty power. I sincerely believe that if we speak of God's wonders of old as documented in the scriptures, coupled with our personal encounters of salvation and deliverance with our children, their faith and love for God will deepen.

Daniel

Daniel was one of the Israelites taken captive in Babylon—a city that had no regard for God, filled with idolatry and all manner of abomination. He was among the young men selected to serve in the king's palace and appointed a daily provision of the king's delicacies and of the wine that the king drank. The Bible records in Daniel 1:8, *"But Daniel purposed in his heart that he would not defile himself with the portion of the king's delicacies, nor with the wine which he drank; therefore he requested of the chief of eunuchs that he might not defile himself."* What audacity! What on earth would give a slave such guts and courage? He should be happy that he had the privilege of eating the same meal and drinking the same wine with the king; instead, he purposed in his heart not to defile himself with the king's delicacies and drink.

Did you ever wonder why he had to do this? Was it necessary? After all, he was a slave in Babylon and should have every reason to enjoy every given opportunity to live differently from how he had lived in Israel. I sincerely believe that Daniel's stand was rooted in the knowledge he had of who he is in God, the promises of God, and Who God is. This knowledge empowered him to take a step of faith in requesting of the king's eunuch not to serve them the king's delicacies and drink. Instead, they should be served vegetables and water. God granted Daniel favour before the eunuch, who served them vegetables and water for ten days as a test to see how they would be affected. The Bible records in verse 15, *"And at the end of ten days their features appeared better and fatter in flesh than all the young men who ate the portion of the king's delicacies."*

The knowledge Daniel had of God that empowered him to make the decision became obvious in the following verses after God revealed Nebuchadnezzar's dream to him in a night vision earlier in chapter 2 of the book of Daniel. in Daniel 2:20-23. Daniel answered and said: *"Blessed be the name of God forever and ever, for wisdom and might are His. And He changes the times and seasons; He removes kings and raises up kings; He gives wisdom to the wise and knowledge to those who have understanding. He reveals deep and secret things; He knows what is in the darkness, and light dwells with Him. I thank You and praise You, O God of my fathers; You have given me wisdom and might, and have now made known to me what we asked of You, for You have made known to us the king's demand."*

Daniel understood that it is God Who raises a king and puts another down; he was convinced that even if the eunuch insisted on giving them the king's delicacies, either God would change the eunuch or remove the king. What mattered to Daniel was obedience to God's law not to defile himself. He knew that God knows the thoughts of his heart. Since he is determined not to defile himself, he was confident that God would do anything to ensure that what he purposed in his heart would come to pass — and that is absolute trust in God. How many of us today are quick to compromise in order to access certain favours from people in authority?

His determination to be obedient to God continued throughout his stay in Babylon, of not wanting to sin against God even though he was in a foreign land. When the governors and satraps were intimidated by Daniel's excellent performance in their kingdom, they did all they could to plot against him, but they could find nothing except for his crazy love for God. The Bible records in Daniel 6:5-10, *then these men said, "We shall not find any charge against this Daniel unless we find it against him concerning the law of His God." So these governors and satraps thronged before the king, and said thus to him: "King Darius, live forever! All governors of the kingdom, and administrators and satraps, the counsellors and advisors, have consulted together to establish a royal statute and to make a firm decree, that whoever petitions any god or man for thirty days, except you, O king, shall be cast into the den of lions. Now, O king, establish the decree and sign the writing, so that it cannot be changed, according to the law of the Medes and Persians, which does not alter. Therefore king Darius signed the written decree. Now when Daniel knew that the writing was signed, he went home. And in his upper room, with his windows open toward Jerusalem, he knelt down on his knees three times that day, and prayed and gave thanks before his God, as this was his custom since early days."*

My good God! Daniel did not need to hide before praying. His windows were opened towards Jerusalem. He knew they would see him, but he was persuaded that the eyes of the Lord were upon Him. This is the life of faith we are called into; however, we have yet to get there because our hearts have not been captured like Daniel's. He loved the Lord to the point that unbelievers knew that his lifestyle was patterned after the law of his God—and they used it against him. Daniel was kept in the lions' den, but the lions could not tamper with him.

Please, read with me as we continue to see how one young man's love for God made an entire kingdom issue a decree for its people to bow to the Lord. See Daniel 6:19-27: *"Then the king arose very early in the morning and went in haste to the den of lions. And when he came to the den, he cried out with a lamenting voice to Daniel. The king spoke, saying to Daniel, 'Daniel, servant of the living God, has your God, whom you serve continually, been able to deliver you from the lions?' Then Daniel said to the king, 'O king, live forever! My God sent His angel and shut the lions' mouths, so that they have not hurt me because I was found innocent before Him; and also, O king, I have done no wrong before you.' Now the king was exceedingly glad for him, and commanded that they should take Daniel up out of the den. So, Daniel was taken up out of the den and no injury whatsoever was found on him, because he believed in his God. And the king gave the command and they brought those men who had accused Daniel and they cast them into the den of lions – them, their children, and their wives; and the lions overpowered them, and broke all their bones in pieces before they ever came to the bottom of the den. Then, king Darius wrote:*

"To all peoples, nations, and languages that dwell in all the earth: peace be multiplied to you. I make a decree that in every dominion of my kingdom men must tremble and fear before the God of Daniel. For He is the living God, and steadfast forever; His kingdom is the one which shall not be destroyed, and His dominion shall endure to the end. He delivers and rescues, and He

works signs and wonders in heaven and on earth, who has delivered Daniel from the power of the lions."

Many of us are not bold enough to stand for God because we have yet to comprehend Who He is. There is something about knowing the Lord for Who He is; it gets one drunken for Him in absolute conviction. Reading through the lives of the saints of old, I understand what the Bible means by *"the just shall live by faith"* (see Romans 1:17 and others), and I have come to the conclusion that genuine faith is born out of love for the Lord. In the midst of challenges, at times our faith seems to be failing us; but if it is built on a foundation of a heart captured by God—that is, in love with God—our faith will always be powered back to life by the fire of our love for God. Without love for God, faith is powerless, unproductive, and cannot stand the test of time.

We do not know what we lose when we do not give our hearts to the Lord. We allow ourselves to go through unnecessary suffering, pain, confusion, and failure. Of all the men discussed in this chapter who stood for God because of their fervent love for Him; from King David to the apostle Paul, Nehemiah, and Daniel, we see that their lives agree with the words of Daniel: *"…the people who know their God shall be strong, and carry out great exploits"* (Daniel 11:32). Their lives also agree with the words of the apostle Paul in 1 Corinthians 2:9, which states, *"Eye has not seen, nor ear heard, nor have entered into the heart of man, the things which God has prepared for those that love Him."*

David was a great king in his time. Paul wrote two-thirds of the New Testament compared with the other apostles. Nehemiah became a governor after serving as the king's cupbearer, and Daniel prospered in the land of captivity. No genuine lover of God ends up a nonentity, but a star for all to see.

Through Our Testimonies and Those of Others

God can also be revealed to us through the testimonies of others. We also witness His mighty works in our lives. Just as we read above, Daniel and other people from biblical times knew of God from His testimonies, in His word, and their own personal experiences.

No person has ever been captured by the wonders of God who does not seek more of God. In the second chapter of my book, *Real Babes Love Jesus*, I wrote testimonies of three young ladies who had transformed lives after an encounter with the love of God through His word of life. Their stories follow:

I will call the first lady Esther. This lady attends one of the churches in Nigeria, whenever she decided to go. She sneaked into the toilet to snort cocaine before the service on any Sunday morning—and sometimes during night vigil. Having been noticed by some sanctuary keepers, the men decided to talk with her since the women were scared of approaching her. On a fateful Sunday morning, she was caught in the act. While she was being taken to the counselling unit, she began to weep about how her life was messed up. With spiritual sensitivity, she was counselled and was told about the love God has for her. She surrendered her life to Jesus and was delivered from that demonic stronghold.

The second one is a lady I will call Bidemi. She is an old friend of mine; I knew the manner of life she had lived. I summoned up courage to ask her questions about her life. She told me how she had lived recklessly in pursuit of pleasure, and what later became of her. According to her, she became inseparable from alcohol and kept late nights. In her words, "If it is not past twelve midnight, it's too early to go home to sleep." The excessive alcohol intake also made her fat.

She told me she had been going to church since childhood. Like the parable of the sower, she heard the word of God, but Satan always came to steal it from her. One night, she got tired. Alcohol, men, and late nights no longer satisfied her. She decided within herself, without anyone preaching to her, to get serious with her life. For the first time in almost thirty years, the word of God penetrated her mind, heart, and soul—destroying the yoke in her life. She gave her life to Christ, fell in love with Jesus, and the reality of the damage alcohol had done to her body hit her. She attended a Bible school, changed her lifestyle, and told me how different she felt—and how she hated all she had done in the past.

The third story is a testimony shared in one of the Sunday services in my church. I am compelled to share it to help someone reading this book. I will call this lady Sheila. She is a young lady who involved herself in all forms of atrocities you could think of. She was a prostitute, a thief, a lesbian, a party freak, and a masturbator. One fateful day she came to church on a Sunday morning, and the cleansing word of God found her and changed her life. She gave her life to Jesus Christ, attended a Bible school, and became a new person entirely. It was such a dramatic intervention and change of life that she could not keep it to herself; she decided to share her story. This is what God can do with human hearts that are yearning for change.

I myself met Jesus in the midst of life challenges, after being disappointed by several loved ones and friends. I have loved and lost and been abused and abandoned. I remember vividly being seated at the old auditorium of Daystar Christian Centre at Oregun, Ikeja, downcast and depressed. No one had invited me to church; I just left the house to see what was happening in that church that attracted such a crowd. I didn't know it, but I was in for an encounter of a lifetime. Pastor Sam Adeyemi preached as though he knew me too well. At the end of the sermon, he spoke about the love of God that rescues us from destruction—and the hand of the enemy. I stood and heeded the call of salvation. As I matured in the faith and studied the word of God, my life changed gradually from the inside—even though there was no immediate physical or material change. I had peace and emotional stability. I have confidence that I am loved beyond measure and secure in the arms of my Beloved. I no longer looked for love in the wrong places; my delight was in the love of God. The Lord gradually dealt with me by His Spirit, and He is still showing me who He is, and His delights.

My life reached a point where nothing mattered but God. For the first time, I found a love that I could trust with my life and future. I have had people in my life who claimed to love me and made promises to help me fulfill my dreams. But on the very verge of destiny fulfillment, they left me without saying goodbye. Meeting with God in His word watered my soul with much encouragement and faith. I grew to love Him in the midst of difficult times; there were times I cried out like Jesus did: *"Father, why have you forsaken me?"* (Matthew 27:46). Then I go back to His word. I read the words of people like Job, in Job 13:15: *"Though He slay me, yet will I trust Him. Even so, I will defend my own ways before Him."* My eyes turned away from my expectations from God to His expectations of me. Labouring in His word, and during worship and prayers, I found myself changing from within until it became visible. I remember telling one of my pastors that, like Job, I had resolved to wait till my time—or change—comes. We will talk more about this in the next chapter on growing in the love of God.

These testimonies and those of other people we know tell

of the dramatic changes the love of God can bring about in people's lives. This helps to strengthen and encourage us to continually abide in Him.

Our individual testimonies are products of divine love and mercy. When I think of the mighty deeds of God in my life, I cannot help but weep in appreciation of His love. He brought me out of Islam into Christianity by His grace, rescued me from sin, and delivered me from the spirit of death. He never allowed the enemy to shoot his evil arrow of the spirit of madness into my life. God stopped it from manifesting in my life. My being alive and well today is by the abundance of His love and mercy. In all of these experiences, I saw God in His loving and caring nature. All of these have endeared my heart to the Lord forever.

From Creation

Psalm 19:1-2 says, *"The heavens declare the glory of God; and the firmaments show His handiwork. Day unto day utters speech, and night unto night reveals knowledge."*

When we look at all the works of God, from the sand on the floor to the muddy ground during the rainy season, to the stars, the moon, the delicate flowers and different kinds of animals; to the different colours, shapes, and sizes of men and women; of different tribes and languages, you cannot help but bow for the God whose wisdom created all of that. I remember during my younger sister's wedding, I was inside the house while my mother was looking for me outside; then, she ran after one of my younger sister's friends, Bunmi, thinking it was me. Even when the lady tried to let my mum know that she was not me, my mum was still speaking our language to her. Because the lady and I look so much alike, you would not believe that we are not related in any way. So, we call each other "my look-alike."

I have had so many reasons to ponder life and everything around me. I have had times when I questioned if God was real or not, especially during my period of persecution after my conversion from Islam to Christianity. At times, when life hurts and no one is there for me, I ask questions daily. My answers came from studying my body, my hair, and all my feminine features, as they differ from those of a man. There were times I walked out of my flat to the main road just to stare at the sky. I remember a particular day. It was about to rain; the clouds were dark and thick outside, and I went out as usual to observe the weather. This time, I got a rude shock. I thought it was going to rain because the clouds were thick. As soon as I looked up—before I knew what was happening—the atmosphere changed in a moment; the cloud regressed like a folded cloth. I was dazed. Another episode occurred when I was to attend a birthday party with a friend. The sun was shining brilliantly and the temperature very high; there was no sign of rainfall. We left for the party. Within a few minutes, there was a heavy downpour, but the sun was still very hot and shining brilliantly—as it was before the rain started. I told my friend, "I fear God." I needed no one to answer my questions; I got my answers from God's creation because no human being has the power to control God's creation; only He alone can do it. I believe if we quiet our souls to listen to what nature says to us daily, we would learn more about God. We would know that He is a beautiful, colourful, and peaceful God. We would find out that He is creative, loving, and much more.

2. Having a Pure Heart

A pure heart is part of the foundational requirements of loving God. We must keep our hearts pure— completely devoid of negative, doubtful thoughts, hatred, and bitterness. The Bible says the pure in heart shall see God; to see God, we must abide in love. This is a ready heart that receives the word of God and obeys it; the type of heart David the Psalmist describes in Psalm 51:16-17: *"For You do not desire sacrifice, or else I would give it; You do not delight in burnt offering. The sacrifices of God are a broken spirit, a broken and a contrite heart – These, O God, You will not despise."* This is the type of heart that is prepared to receive the word of God; it can be tickled and captured by it, unlike a stony heart.

3. Acceptance of His Love as an Invitation for an Eternal Affair

The Bible is a personal love letter from the Lord. It shows us how much God loves us that He gave His only begotten son just to reconcile us back to Himself. The love God bestowed on us cost Him His dear Son. The Bible tells us that we were bought with a price. Our life is no longer ours, but of the Lord (1 Corinthians 6:20). That is why Jesus said that we have not chosen Him, but He chose us.

When we accept this love of God and begin to see Him as He really is, it becomes easy to relate to Him. When our love for God is real and approached with the same intensity at which we go about our earthly relationships, we will begin to enjoy another dimension of life. An intimate affair with the Lord is so sweet that it cannot be compared with our hyped carnal relationships; it is so real that we will not want to be with anyone but Him.

There was a day I was forced to ask a friend of mine if I would ever be able to risk my love for the Lord for my earthly relationships, since my heart had been captured by the love of the Lord. My friend told me I would be able to, not in the worldly way, but in a better way because the Holy Spirit would empower it. The Lord began to teach me how to be an extension of His love to others. Most of what you are reading in this book is my personal experience of God's dealing with me in the school of divine love. When we are able to define the love of God as being superior to our earthly pervasive relationships, it becomes easy for love to flow from our hearts to the Lord. Pleasing Him would become our number-one goal.

4. Accepting, Living, and Walking in the Grace of God

We must never forget that it was the grace of God that located us for salvation; that must never be taken for granted. The grace of God is what saves us from our sin, even when we do not deserve it.

When we consciously walk in the grace of God by totally accepting what it carries, we will not struggle to love and obey God. When we realise that we are not of ourselves and can do nothing without the grace of God, our trust in Him deepens. Paul the apostle said in 1 Corinthians 15:10, *"But by the grace of God I am what I am, and His grace toward me was not in vain; but I laboured more abundantly than they all, yet not I, but the grace of God which was with me."*

We cannot love God without His grace. We cannot live right and achieve anything meaningful in life without the grace of God. Many people believe that Jesus has died for all our sins; hence, they can still walk in sin. But they have forgotten the scripture that says, *"Shall we continue in sin that grace may abound?"* (Romans 6:1). The answer is no. If we truly love the Lord, we will accept the grace of God, which empowers us to obey God in order to abide in His love. Grace is a good teacher and a good friend of our conscience, because His grace is the expression of His love to us. Titus 2:11–12 says, *"For the grace of God that brings salvation has appeared to all men, teaching us that, denying ungodliness and worldly lusts, we should live soberly, righteously, and godly in the present age."*

Without grace we cannot reach out to others; we cannot express the love of God in our hearts to Him and the world around us. Living and walking in grace is the determination to extend ourselves to others in uncommon ways even when they do not deserve it. This makes them see God in their lives and situation. We should correct others—without being judgmental—through the lenses of our lives and what we are going through. Every time we reach out to someone else in grace, life stretches its arms of grace out to us.

What Loving God Does for Us:

1. We become fruitful (John 15:4-9).
2. We become joyful (John 15:11).
3. We become His friend—like Abraham—whom He shares His secrets with (John 15:15).
4. We are empowered to witness for Him (John 15:26-27).
5. We will be full of light (1 John 1:5).
6. We become God's habitation (John 14:23).
7. We enjoy His peace (John 14:27).
8. All of God becomes ours—and ours, His.
9. It births a spirit of unity in our hearts; if we love God, we will desire to be one with those who love Him as well (John 17:21-23).
10. Loving God makes us "rapturable."

What Loving Others Will Do for Us:

1. Our lives are enriched.
2. We are happier.
3. We attract more grace and resources from the Lord.

4. We feel more at peace and connected to the entire creation.

What Loving Others Will Do for Them:

1. They feel loved and accepted.
2. They appreciate God and life.
3. We become a testimony in their lives by validating the goodness of our God.
4. We make God real in their hearts.
5. We make the world a better place for them to live.
6. We impart to them the grace to become agents of good as well.

Chapter Four

Growing in the Love of God

"The cause of Christ can be painful and costly. It is about sacrifice. But the sacrifice is motivated by love, not fear. And the love is what sets us free." - Jeanette Thomason

We read earlier how the *"love of God has been shed abroad in our hearts by the Holy Spirit"* (Romans 5:5). Though His love is already poured in our hearts, we have our own role to play to activate and walk in this divine love. Our part is the willingness to grow in the love of God. Coming to the saving knowledge of God is not enough; it is the beginning of our spiritual journey with God. The Bible enjoins us to work out our salvation with fear and trembling (Philippians 2:12).

Understanding that love is the foundation of the Christian journey and the end of it should spur us to pursue it with all we have. 1 Corinthians 13:13 says, *"And now abide faith, hope, love, these three; but the greatest of these is love."* While 1 John 4:17 states, *"Love has been perfected among us in this: that we may have boldness in the day of judgment; because as He is, so are we in this world."* Love is the greatest. Faith and hope are the means to the end — which is our being with the Lord forever — but love is that end. Perfection in love is what makes us ready and gives us boldness on Judgment Day when we get to heaven; we would not need hope and faith anymore but will be dwelling in love. Alleluia!

While we are here on earth, it is the love of God in our hearts that keeps us going, even when all seems to be failing us. When we cannot understand what the present is saying, we rest in the word of our Beloved, when He said: *"I will never leave you nor forsake you"* (Hebrews 13:5).

How Do I Grow in the Love of God?

1. Total Surrender of the Heart to the Lord

To grow in the love of God, the next thing to do after salvation is to surrender and totally yield our hearts to God. Jesus said that if a person desires to build a house, he or she should count the cost before embarking on the project (see Luke 14:28). The same applies to us in our divine relationship with the Lord. It is important to note that our relationship with the Lord is one that demands us to submit our entire lives and beings into His hands. It is a covenant relationship with specific terms. The prerequisite is to lose our lives in order to gain them. Until we lose them, our hearts cannot be empty of all the junk from the world that we are carrying into God's kingdom. We have to surrender all we once thought was right; all we once desired, hoped for, and lived for to the scrutiny of God. This is what surrender is all about. This would make it easy for us to gradually grow to be like-minded with our Beloved and not be offended in Him or think that He is altering our lives thereby, rebel against Him. Jesus said in Luke 14:33, *"So likewise, whoever of you does not forsake all that he has cannot be My disciple."* And in Luke 16:13, *"No servant can serve two masters; for either he will hate the one and love the other, or else he will be loyal to the one and despise the other. You cannot serve God and mammon."* Until our hearts are absolutely given to God, we cannot love Him enough to subject every other affection under His authority. We must note that:

A. God cannot use us if our hearts are not totally yielded to Him.

B. Only a yielded heart can be trained His way.

C. Only a surrendered heart can be humble enough to become nothing before the Lord.

D. Only someone with a yielded heart would lay his or her life on God's altar to be crucified with Christ. This would be till humanity is swallowed up, and Christ—the hope of glory—is formed in him or her.

E. It takes a surrendered heart to take the word of God for what it is without questioning or reasoning it out.

F. Only a yielded heart can walk in faith and trust God implicitly as the only wise and all-knowing guide.

2. Becoming a Living Sacrifice

Being a living sacrifice is the life of the surrendered heart in action. The proof that our hearts are yielded to the Lord is in our lifestyle, which is the fruit of a surrendered life. The Bible enjoins us in Romans 12:1-2, *"I beseech you therefore, brethren, by the mercies of God, that you present your bodies a living sacrifice, holy, acceptable to God, which is your reasonable service. And do not be conformed to this world, but be transformed by the renewing of your mind, that you may prove what is that good and acceptable and perfect will of God."*

What does it mean to be a living sacrifice? We are living sacrifices when we allow God by His Spirit to do the work of the cross in our hearts, which in turn dictates how we live our lives daily. It is a process of death in which flesh is mortified and the life of God is manifested in us. The Bible makes us understand that if we love the world, the love of the Father is not in us; the Bible enumerates the manifestation of those things that are of the world which we should *not* love, as mentioned in the previous chapter: the lust of the flesh, the lust of the eyes, and the pride of life (1 John 2:16). These are the key issues we need to deal with in our lives in order to be able to grow in the love of God. If we do not deal with them, they will choke our love for the Lord. And, as in the parable of the sower (Matthew 13:1-23), the cares of this world will make us unfruitful (verse 22).

What are these things of the world that we need to die to? Men and women are made up of the body, the soul, and the spirit. The spirits of men and women are real; they communicate with the world through their souls. Their bodies are the cases through which actions are carried out. When we get born again, the Spirit of God regenerates our spirits, but our souls and bodies are still the same. The battle of our relationship with the Lord is warfare that goes on in our souls and bodies. Our souls are made up of the mind, the willpower, and the emotions. This is where the devil always thrives because a lot of us are not properly guided on how to submit our souls to the Lord as well. I suffered a great deal in this area because I am an emotional person. But I learnt the hard way because God needed to draw my attention to it in a very painful way. He taught me how to be stable in my walk with Him.

As a believer and a child of God, the devil is after your mind, your will, and your emotions. If he can have these three, he will paralyse your relationship with God. I am sure you are wondering why and how. Yes, when we do not renew our minds with the word of God to align our thinking with God's thoughts, we open ourselves to be misguided and to be led by false visions, voices, and counsel. In aligning our minds with God's word, we begin to understand His will for our lives. As we do that, His will becomes our will; we no longer want to do things our way, but God's way. As we proceed, we learn to live by faith as children of God and not by feelings. As we learn this, we realise that most times the way we feel does not necessarily reflect the true nature of things or the mind of God. The devil operates in the realm of the physical and the flesh; the Bible says the flesh profits nothing but the Spirit gives life (John 6:63). If we do not renew our minds by the word of God and allow the Spirit behind the word of God to impart strength in our inner selves, we will not be able to resist the devil; likewise, we will not be able to have a stable relationship with God.

For instance, if you have a friend, you pray together and do things in common. If this relationship helps your personal prayer life and life generally, the enemy will not be happy. He will begin to make you see faults in your friend, and most of the time the devil uses an aspect of your life that is yet to receive the light of God. Before you know it, you will begin to pick faults and misunderstanding comes in. This might truncate your praying together and invariably affect your prayer life and your friend's prayer life. When you live in the Spirit, as soon as such thoughts come into your mind, you will begin to plead the body and blood of Christ and intercede for your friend concerning it. And discuss the issue with him or her at the appropriate time, as led by the Lord.

This is why the Bible enjoins us in Galatians 5:16-18, "*I say then: Walk in the Spirit, and you shall not fulfill the lust of the flesh. For the flesh lusts against the Spirit, and the Spirit against the flesh; and these are contrary to one another, so that you do not do the things that you wish. When you are led by the Spirit, you are not under the law.*" Living and walking in God's love is living and walking in the Spirit. We have to personally work to build our inner selves by the help of the Holy Spirit. If our inner selves are weak, our souls and bodies will take over. It takes strength from the inner person to say no to sin. I love the way Roberts Liardon puts it in his book, *Run to the Battle*. He said, "The anointing is not meant for our practical everyday living. Strength of character, the authority of the inner man—the human spirit—gives us the ability to resist temptation and do what is right every day. The anointing does not help you resist sin." Immediately, when I read this portion of his book, my spirit responded. I wrote in the margin: "This is what the word of God and speaking in tongues do for us; they strengthen our inner man."

If the Spirit leads us, we are not under the law because being led by the Spirit puts us under the cover of the grace of God—the grace that teaches and empowers us to shun ungodliness even when no one is seeing us, or it is born out of the holy fear of the Lord. Galatians 6:17 says, *"From now on let no one trouble me, for I bear in my body the marks of the Lord Jesus."* How did Paul the apostle come to bear the marks of Christ upon Him? He partook of the cross of Jesus—the working of the cross in a surrendered heart. If we are not dead to the world, we cannot be alive to God. Unsaved men and women cannot love God. This is the mystery of the resurrection power. The cross is our hope as Christians. If we proclaim we love God, but we are not yielded to Him by carrying our cross and glorying in His cross, where is the love we proclaim? Where is the honour we proclaim?

We can never be made perfect in the body of dust and the pride in us. It is at the cross that our love for God is tested and perfected. It is at the cross, in God's fire of refinement, that we are empowered to obey God's word and be able to abide in His love. It is in this place we discover that we are nothing but dirt and nothing good is in us, which births hunger and desire to seek for that which is good — and that is God. It is in living out this surrendered life that we discover how much God loves us. He can rescue us from the destruction of the world and the evil that is in it. This takes us into a deeper level of existence where the reality of life in God is made evident to us.

If we do not surrender to become living sacrifices, we cannot grow in the love of God. If we do not grow in His love, we cannot be faithful to Him; if we are not faithful to Him, we cannot experience the fullness of what He has in store for us. And this truncates the indescribable joy that is our lot in Him, making us live defeated lives. Our depth in God is determined by how much we are willing for Him to do the work of the cross in us; only our depth will take us far in the Christian journey, make us meaningful, and preserve our Christian testimony. Like Enoch, we walk with the Lord (Genesis 5:22-24). Read 2 Corinthians 5:14-15, which says, *"For the love of Christ compels us, because we judge thus: that if One died for all, then all died; and He died for all, that those who live should live no longer for themselves, but for Him who died for them and rose again."* Alleluia!

3. Studying and Obeying His Word

The Bible enjoins us in Colossians 3:16: *"Let the word of Christ dwell in you richly in all wisdom, teaching and admonishing one another in psalms and hymns and spiritual songs, singing with grace in your hearts to the Lord."* The word of God is God. John 1:1 says, *"In the beginning was the Word, and the Word was with God, and the Word was God."* When we study the word, we feast on Jesus. The more we fellowship with the Lord in His word, the more our love for Him deepens, especially when we are able to relate with all that is written and we are able to get direction and guidance. We also find answers to questions that have troubled our hearts. Reading through the scriptures reveals our hearts to us as human beings and how long God has been merciful to humankind in spite of our sins and outright rebellion against Him. As we see the heart of God poured out to us through the eyes of the scriptures, we cannot help but respond to Him.

Even more so, the Bible says in 2 Corinthians 3:3, "*Clearly you are an epistle of Christ, ministered by us, written not with ink but by the Spirit of the living God, not on tablets of stone but on tablets of flesh, that is, of the heart.*" If we are epistles of Christ written with the Spirit of the living God, it means that the more of God's word we have in us, the more the Spirit of God uses it to sync our spirits with the Lord. If the Lord is love, then, the more we take on His Spirit, and the more we grow in love.

As we study His word, our faith in Him grows; we move from mere believing to trusting Him that He is whom He says He is. He will not fail us—as some people do or have done to us in the past. In trusting Him, it becomes easy to obey His word without question.

The truth is that knowing His word is not enough; we must be *doers* of His word. We must obey Him by taking heed to His word. This is what we mean by attuning our lives to His. The surrendered life has no means of existence other than obeying God's authority; that is where our protection and abiding in His love is. Jesus said in John 14:23-24, "*If anyone loves Me, he will keep My word; and My Father will love him, and We will come to him and make Our home with him. He who does not love Me does not keep My words; and the word which you hear is not Mine but the Father's who sent Me.*" If we truly love the Lord, we will obey His word. In doing that we will become His habitation. We will be abiding in

His everlasting love. But if we claim to love Him and do not obey Him, we lie — and the truth is not in us.

We must continually, by God's grace, labour in His word and obey Him in order to continually grow and abide in His love.

4. Spending Quality Time in Prayer

The altar of prayer is an altar of change. Prayer is God's workshop for heart transplants and transformations. In the place of prayer, we commune with God. We get to know His mind and feelings towards our specific situations and us. Jeremiah 33:3 says: *"Call unto Me, and I will answer you, and show you great and mighty things, which you do not know."* It is what we know that empowers us, and as we read in earlier chapters, the revelation of Who God is births eternal purpose in our hearts. It is only in the place of prayer that we get revelation from God. Therefore, we must raise altars for God in our homes and places of work, while we ourselves become mobile altars. As we drive or walk around, our steps are anointed of the Lord; the words that proceed from our mouth are graciously emanating the love of God.

God is a Spirit. As spiritual people, our speeches should become prayer no matter where we are. Prayer softens our hearts towards God and humankind. In prayer, we know God's plan for our nation, His kingdom, and us. In prayer we are quickened by God's Spirit; our broken hearts are mended and our fears are cast out because perfect love cast out fear (1 John 4:18). Every battle of the flesh is won on our knees because every instance of warfare we fight or engage in is a battle from the pit of hell to stop us from doing the will of God so that we do not abide in His love — our stronghold. And if we lose this battle we become prey to the devil. God forbid. Alleluia!

5. Praise and Worship God in the Beauty of His Holiness

From my experience of God, I found that this is really the place of expressing our feelings to the Lord. The truth is that in the beginning of our walk with God, it looks dry, and we initially come short of what to tell Him or the song to sing to Him. But as we press on and He begins to reveal Himself to us through His mighty acts of deliverance and peace, songs naturally come out of our hearts to Him. I also came to the realisation that it is beyond just singing to the Lord; our lives could be lived in such a way that it spurs others to praise God. This is a life of sacrifice, laying all we are and have become at God's altar to minister to Him who owns us. All we have is the beginning of our worship to Him.

At the altar of praise our choice of songs is very important; the focus must be Him and Him alone. Whether we like the song or not, it is not about us, but the Lord. I discovered that most of the songs we like to sing only excite our flesh; not our spirits. We must learn to sing to the Lord. Get a hymnbook and read psalms to Him; you will be glad you did. I have a hymnbook by my bedside. Sometimes, when I do not know what to do, I just pick a hymn and sing it aloud. All of these actions make our relationship with the Lord real.

Our response to His word when the verses tickle us during study is a mode of worship. I remember times when I would be studying the word and I would burst into laughter. I would hear myself say, "Yes Lord, You are good." Sometimes, I just write in the margin of my Bible, "God, you are too much." All these are acts of worship spurred from believing in the integrity of His word. Every time we do this, something happens in the spirit realm between God and us—and ultimately inside us. It is here that we can behold His throne like Isaiah, and a holy fear is born in our spirits for the one we love. It is at the altar of worship that the Lord reveals our hearts to us and teaches us how to reverence Him.

There was a time in my life that I needed more of God. The state of my heart was cloudy, and I felt a strain between the Lord and myself. As I was praying, I suddenly switched to praise and worship. It was as if the Lord had been waiting for me. I felt fire burning in my heart; afterward, I received clarity, fresh fire, anointing, and His grace. The more of His grace we receive, the more our capacity to love Him increases and the more of His glory our lives express.

6. Meditating on the Cross of Calvary

I believe if we keep what transpired at the cross as a memorial in our hearts, we will grow in the love of God. When we find ourselves in situations beyond us that make us question God's love, we must remember the cross. This is what Hebrews 12:2-3 reminds us: *"[L]ooking unto Jesus, the author and finisher of our faith, who for the joy that was set before Him endured the cross, despising the shame, and has sat down at the right hand of the throne of God."* Jesus endured the cross in obedience to the will of God. He saw you and me redeemed from the hand of the enemy. It cost Him separation from the Father. He went through much suffering because of us. Our own is a light affliction that is working for our good to enter into the victory His love has won for us. This will help us to go through any situation in our personal life or place of calling. That is a love built on a solid foundation. The cross is an invisible emblem of love that we must carry in our hearts; it reminds us of one word: SACRIFICE, which perpetually puts us at a place of love. Colossians 2:14-15 says, *"…having wiped out the handwriting of requirements that was against us, which was contrary to us. And He has taken it out of the way, having nailed it to the cross. Having disarmed principalities and powers, He made a public spectacle of them, triumphing over them in it."*

7. A Life of Sacrificial Giving

The more we give to the Lord and support His cause, the more our hearts are steadfast in Him because where our treasure is there our hearts will be (Matthew 6:21). We see this happened in the life of Abraham, the man described in the Bible as the friend of God. He was tested by God to know how much love he has for Him because it was God's plan to enter into an everlasting covenant with him. God asked him to sacrifice his only son, the Isaac he has waited for, whom the Bible said Abraham did not stagger at the promise for (Romans 4:20). That same child God said he should sacrifice, but Abraham believed in his heart that love does no wrong. He believed that if the Lord required of him Isaac, then his Lover had a better plan to either resurrect Isaac or give to him another Isaac because he believed in the faithfulness of his Lover and Friend. While Isaac was laid on the altar, the Lord truly provided for Himself a lamb for the sacrifice. After this, He entered into an everlasting covenant with Abraham. Genesis 22:15-18 reads: *"Then the Angel of the LORD called to Abraham a second time out of heaven, and said: 'By Myself I have sworn, says the LORD, because you have done this thing, and have not withheld your son, your only son — blessing I will bless you, and multiplying I will multiply your descendants as the stars of the heaven and as the sand which is on the seashore; and your descendants shall possess the gate of their enemies. In your seed all the nations of the earth shall be blessed, because you have obeyed My voice.'"*

The truth is, the more we live a life of sacrificial giving to God and humankind, the more of His faithfulness we experience and the more our hearts are endeared to Him as we continually experience His faithfulness.

8. Cultivating a Life of Patient Life

Nothing helps us to mature in the love of God like patient faith. A patient faith is a faith that hopes against hope, glorying in the Lord like Abraham. Oftentimes in our relationship with God, we wonder why certain things happened to us in spite of our faith in God. Why the delay of the promise? Maybe you are reading this book and you have a sick child; or you are sick yourself; or your business has been stagnating—and you are wondering why, in spite of your love and commitment to the Lord. Do not quit! Do not complain. He still loves you, and His word is true in your life. He said that even if a nursing mother forgets her child, He *"will not forget you"* (Isaiah 49:15). If you do not quit, and you pray and praise Him more, you will discover more truth about God and yourself. As you continually lean on Him and shift your focus from your situation to His word and Him, miracles will begin to happen without you asking for them. Amen.

This reminds me of the story of Hannah in the Bible. Her mate ridiculed her for not having a child. Every year, she went to Shiloh to worship and sacrifice to the Lord. She never got tired or gave up, even though it was a time in history when the word of the Lord was scarce. People lived as they desired. Hannah held onto God to the point of making a vow to return to the Lord the child she was asking from Him if her request was granted. From Hannah's song of thanksgiving and praise in 1 Samuel 2:1-2, we see a woman who waited to judge God faithful through a persistent and persevering relationship with the Lord. Hear her words in 1 Samuel 2:1-2, *"My heart rejoices in the LORD; my horn is exalted in the LORD. I smile at my enemies, because I rejoice in Your salva-*

tion. No one is holy like the Lord, *for there is none besides You, nor is there any rock like our God."*

9. Walking in the Fear of the Lord

The truth is that our obedience cannot be total if we do not have the fear of God in our hearts. The fear of God I am talking about is not the fear that paralyses, because perfect love casts out fear (1 John 4:18). It is reverence for God that He is holy and sovereign. You will agree with me after reading through the story of King David that what helped him to sustain His love for the Lord and get back on track every time he failed or disobeyed the Lord was his holy fear and reverence for God and His power. I am afraid that these days many of us don't have reverence for the Lord; this reflects in our attitudes towards Him in places of worship and especially in our secret lives. The story of Joseph in the Bible is a typical example of a man who fears the Lord. Joseph would have slept with Potiphar's wife without the knowledge of anyone (see Genesis chapter 39), but there was a light in His heart; it was the light of God born out of a holy fear for God. No wonder Joseph said, *"I fear God"* (Genesis 42:18).

In my personal life, I have found myself in situations that seemed like an open ticket to sin because no one would see me. But I have been taught by the Holy Spirit that there are no walls in the spiritual realm and that the eyes of the Lord run to and fro to show Himself mighty on behalf of those who fear Him. The consciousness and belief in the omnipresence of God birthed in me a deep, marked reverence in my soul not to want to knowingly do anything that will displease Him. As I continue to live in this consciousness. I became more at home with the Lord than with the people around me. His love grew in my heart, and my relationship with Him became a reality.

Chapter Four

Why It Seems Difficult for People to Grow in God's Love

1. COVETOUSNESS/MATERIALISM

We are in the times where people no longer live by faith but by sight because the enemy has created an atmosphere that promotes materialism and a get-all-you-can-quickly attitude. We read in Luke 12:13–15 of a man who pleaded with Jesus to help him collect his inheritance from his brothers. But Jesus, knowing the motive behind the man's request, denied it. There was nothing wrong in the young man asking for his inheritance. I believe that Jesus saw a character flaw in him that created such desperation for his inheritance. Read with me: *"Then one from the crowd said to Him, 'Teacher, tell my brother to divide the inheritance with me.' But He said to him, 'Man, who made Me a judge or an arbitrator over you?' And He said to them, "Take heed and beware of covetousness, for one's life does not consist in the abundance of the things he possesses.' "*

So many people today believe that society and the people in it will only respect them based on what they have; therefore, they spend their entire lives acquiring–and acquiring without being satisfied. There is no end to covetousness. A covetous person cannot be loyal to the Lord; therefore, he or she will not be able to go a long way with God. The words of Luke 16:13 testify to this. The passage says, *"No servant can serve two masters; for either he will hate the one and love the other, or else he will be loyal to the one and despise the other. You cannot serve God and mammon."*

The antidote to covetousness is contentment. 1 Timothy 6:6–10 states, *"Now godliness with contentment is great gain. For we brought nothing into this world, and it is certain we can carry nothing out. And having food and clothing, with these we shall be content. But those who desire to be rich fall into tempta-*

tion and a snare, and into many foolish and harmful lusts which drown men in destruction and perdition. For the love of money is a root of all kinds of evil, for which some have strayed from the faith in their greediness, and pierced themselves through with many sorrows."

2. EARTHLY MINDEDNESS

So many believers have yet to accept their position as heaven dwellers. If we do not believe that we have been raised with Christ and are to live from that place in our physical bodies, our experiences on earth will not be any different from that of an unbeliever. The Bible enjoins us in Colossians 3:1-2, *"If then you were raised with Christ, seek those things which are above, where Christ is, sitting at the right hand of God. Set your mind on things above, not on things on the earth."* If we become heavenly minded, we can be driven by God's love and eternity, and this will help us to grow in the Lord, tremendously abiding in His love. Or else, the cares of this world will choke the love of God in our hearts. When we are so engrossed in what to eat, what to wear, or our children's school fees more than setting our hearts on trusting the Lord, we cheat ourselves and deny ourselves access to what God is saying about those issues that bother us.

We must therefore not allow the cares of this world to get in the way because it has a way of choking God's love in our hearts and stunting us from growing in the Lord. This is why Jesus told His disciples in Luke 12:22-31, *"Therefore I say to you, do not worry about your life, what you will eat; nor about the body, what you will put on. Life is more than food, and the body is more than clothing. Consider the ravens, for they neither sow nor reap, which have neither storehouse nor barn; and God feeds them. Of how much more value are you than the birds? And which of you by worrying can add one cubit to his stature? If you then are not able to do the least, why are you anxious for the rest? Consider the lilies, how they grow: they neither toil nor spin; and yet I say to you, even Solomon in all his glory was not arrayed like one of these. If then God so clothes the grass, which today is in the field and tomorrow is thrown into the oven, how much more will He clothe you, O you of little faith? "And do not seek what you should eat or what you should drink, nor have an anxious mind. For all these things the nations of the world seek after, and your Father knows that you need these things. But seek the kingdom of God, and all these things shall be added to you."*

3. FEAR OF MAN/HONOUR FROM MAN

This is the most tragic reason why people — especially our youths, politicians, and businesspeople — find it difficult to grow in the love of God. For youths, it is the fear of not being accepted amongst their peers if they go the extra mile with God; the fear of being treated as an outcast and of losing those they love to be with. For politicians, it is the fear of not being accepted by political colleagues or allies as being up to the task to deliver. This is why a lot of supposed believers get into politics or political offices and begin to compromise because they have to please people to retain their position of relevance. This is disheartening and sickening; it shows how little we understand the God we serve. Likewise, some businesspeople have business partners that are unbelievers. In order to please them, they compromise their faith by disobeying God — making it impossible for them to abide in the love of God.

Even more so, I have come across people who know the truth about God and Jesus Christ but are afraid of taking a stand for Him because of persecution. Some of these people are professing Christians and quite a number are of other religions. These fears are innumerable. Some fear not getting contracts — as mentioned earlier. It is surprising to note that similar events were recorded in John 12:42-43: *"Never-*

theless even among the rulers many believed in Him, but because of the Pharisees they did not confess Him, lest they should be put out of the synagogue; for they loved the praise of men more than the praise of God."

Jesus has this to say to everyone who fears and honours people more than God. Consider John 5:41–44, *"I do not receive honor from men. But I know you, that you do not have the love of God in you. I have come in My Father's name, and you do not receive Me; if another comes in his own name, him you will receive. How can you believe, who receive honor from one another, and do not seek the honor that comes from the only God?"*

We must therefore seek the honour that comes from the only true God. Amen.

Chapter Five

Experiencing the Reality of God's Love Daily

"Every spiritual believer knows that love should be offered first. Unless love is offered, nothing is offered."- Watchman Nee

Looking at the church today, we see that our definition of and attitude about love has remained myopic, like the people of the world; this is not supposed to be. This is why we have a hard time putting love and emotions into perspective in our daily lives.

I came across some Christian literature on love for young people. From the cover page, I got an impression that love is something we are to keep and reserve for special people in our lives. People find it difficult to dwell in love and love others because they have grown up with this mentality, especially young people. This in turn has caused a lot of young people to drift away from the Lord because they have not been taught to understand love from its very root and be able to identify Jesus as their first love—and how they can live their lives from that foundation every day. It is in understanding God's love and abiding in it that we are empowered to live whole, healthy, and happy lives. Then we will be able to love others.

A vacuum is created in our hearts—and unrealistic expectations from life and people—when we jump the gun to create experiences for ourselves and to love others without having and developing a love relationship with God. In longing to fill this vacuum, we live a life of trial and error; we expose ourselves to unnecessary danger and jump from one relationship to another and from one bad habit to another: such as smoking, alcohol consumption, and increased illicit sexual acts. This is why the Bible says in Proverbs 27:7-8, "*A satisfied soul loathes the honeycomb, but to a hungry soul every bitter thing is sweet. Like a bird that wanders from its nest is a man who wanders from his place.*" Our only satisfaction as designed by God is Him. He remains our place of safety and refuge. If we do not start our lives from Him, we can never get it right. Everything will look good—even when it leads to our destruction.

We read in the Bible the love of God for humanity and how He became man to save us from our sins. It astounds my imagination how the Almighty God could be so bothered about us because of love that He would make such a sacrifice in order to give us an authentic life to live.

We can never appreciate the depth of redemption until we ponder what preceded and happened on the cross of Calvary. What could have made our Lord Jesus Christ go through so much to save us, if not for love? If our hearts are not captured by this truth, we will never fully comprehend the call of God upon our lives. Many of us love to talk about faith because it has to do with God and us; it is personal. But love is not just between God and us; it is what we are called to be, to live daily, in God and for others. We just read in the previous chapter that God is love and that He that dwells in love dwells in God and God in Him (1 John 4:16).

It is important that as Christians we see our relationship with the Lord as one of a love affair. This will help us to guard our Christian walk and our hearts. We are the Bride of Jesus Christ. He is our first love and has enjoined us in Song of Solomon 8:6-7: *"Set me as a seal upon your heart, as a seal upon your arm; for love is as strong as death, jealousy as cruel as the grave; its flames are flames of fire, a most vehement flame. Many waters cannot quench love, nor can the floods drown it. If a man would give for love all the wealth of his house, it will be utterly despised."*

If we set God as a seal upon our hearts and all that is in us, we will obey His word, give ourselves to His cause, and serve Him for Who He is, and not for what we can get from Him. This is why our faith is often tested in trials by God to see if our faith is love rooted and driven or is motivated by the things we hope to get from Him. If we love God, we will spend time with Him in His house and in our private corners daily. We will boldly say, like David, that our delight is to be in the presence of the Lord (Psalm 27:4). If we love Him, we will love our neighbours.

God's Love: The Road to a Happy and Fulfilling Life

When we understand and function in the love of God daily, we live a worry-free life because our hearts will be so endeared to God to believe, trust and obey Him absolutely. Jesus said we should abide in His love by obeying His word; while 1 Peter 5:7 says we should cast all our care upon Him because He cares for us. If we truly believe that God cares for us, we will obey by truly casting it upon Him, thus abiding in His love. True joy and happiness is in abiding in His love. Hear Jesus in John 15:9-11: *"As the Father loved Me, I also have loved you; abide in My love. If you keep My commandments, you will abide in My love, just as I have kept My Father's commandments and abide in His love. These things I have spoken to you, that My joy may remain in you, and that your joy may be full."* What a life! That in simple obedience to the commandments of God, we abide in His love. His joy will be in us—making our joy full.

We are so valuable to God that He wants to rule over all that concerns us; the Bible says in 1 Peter 5:7 that we should cast our cares upon Him because He cares for us. Our understanding of this should calm us down and never cause us to be worried. We can become like the apostle Paul who learnt never to worry about anything. Instead, he learned to be content in all things, whether with much or little, because he understood that he was no longer of himself. He said the life that he lived he lived for Christ (Galatians 2:20).

This same attitude should be in us too, because our life is no longer ours. We have been bought with a price. Like the prophet Habakkuk in verses 3:17-19, we can say: *"Though the fig tree may not blossom, nor fruit be on the vines; though the labour of the olive may fail, and the fields yield no food; though the flock may be cut off from the fold, and there be no herds in the stall — Yet I will rejoice in the LORD, I will joy in the God of my salvation. The LORD God is my strength; he will make my feet like deer's feet, and He will make me walk on my high hills."*

This should be our confession as God's children radically in love with Him for Who He is, no matter what life throws at us or how things are with us in life; our joyful confession of God's love and care will keep us on the path to victory and keep us from backsliding.

I have seen this work in my life, when days, months, and years passed, and it seemed that nothing was progressing around me; it was as if everyone had left me behind because I chose to heed the call of God in my life and refused to live the normal life controlled by people. I was absolutely surrendered to God to lead and take care of me. My case became a prayer point to everyone because some of them thought I did not know what I was doing or that I was under a spell. Some of my friends thought my commitment to the walk of faith with God had taken me from the path of reality; but because I know that the only reality that exists is the reality of God's love that never abandons nor fails, I never allowed any of those comments to alter my joy. I know Whom I believe and that He loves me with an everlasting love; this kept me on the path of peace. I was able to stand my ground in the face of temptations and mockery. Today, the story is different because of the praise of the name of the Lord.

Abiding in the love of God gives us strength and the assurance of what tomorrow holds for us. Even though we do not know what tomorrow holds, we know the God that holds tomorrow in His hands. This mindset and positive confession leads us to rest in the promises of God because we love and trust Him enough. Hebrews 4:9-11 says: *"There remains therefore a rest for the people of God. For he who has entered His rest has himself also ceased from his own work as God did from His. Let us therefore be diligent to enter that rest, lest anyone fall according to the same example of disobedience."*

The love of God births obedience in us because we would not want to hurt but to please the people we love. In turn, this births faith in our hearts, to believe Him because love believes all things. This is our rest in God. This is a place where the grace of God does everything for us at His pace; only love can bring us to that place. From Hebrews 11, we read about the heroes of faith—from Abraham to Enoch to Moses, and so on. These men were committed to God and His purpose for their lives and generation. A life rooted in the love of God is a life of absolute conviction; a life that does not count the cost but endures to the end. It is an enduring relationship that helps us to see Him Who is invisible by faith.

We can never live a fruitful, happy life as Christians if we are not sunken and rooted in the love of God. So many people are frustrated because they have yet to personalise the message of 1 Corinthians chapter 13 in relation to God and humankind. Their love is conditional: I do this for you, and you do this for me. When it's not happening, they become offended in God or with humankind.

Brothers and sisters, we need to retrace our steps and prioritise making first things first in our lives. Even our faith cannot function without love; it must be rooted in the love of God because the Bible says in Galatians 5:6, *"For in Christ Jesus neither circumcision nor uncircumcision avails anything, but faith working through love."*

I have met genuinely nice Christians who still expect reciprocation for every act of kindness they show to people. When their expectations are not met, they get angry, frustrated, and feel cheated. But the God kind of love is not like that; it is unconditional because it is an expression and extension of the invisible God. Only He can repay us if we ever hope for a refund. Can we ever thank God enough for all the love He has showed us—and is still showing us? No! Yet, we do not deserve it. Love is deep, spiritual, and selfless.

As we determinedly abide in His love, we learn patience to wait on Him. We also learn patience in our daily dealings with friends, family, loved ones, and acquaintances. As time goes on, we will understand and be able to interpret the events of our lives, knowing that God is in our corner watching over our affairs. This also helps us to be patient with others—reducing our expectations on them and increasing our expectations on God who commanded us to cast our cares upon Him because the Bible says the expectation of the righteous will not be cut off (Proverbs 23:18).

I understand there are times when we stretch out our hands in love to help people when they don't expect us to. They become suspicious of us, as if the help comes with an ulterior motive or we want something in return. I have experienced this, but such people cannot deter us because it is just a reflection of the state of their hearts and their depth of understanding of God's love. Why are we not suspicious of God's love towards us? For me, when I receive unexpected kindness and love from people, especially strangers, all I see is Jesus. I say to myself, "God has come down through one of His children to help me and to show me how much I am loved and how much He is mindful of me." This happens to me often, enabling me to live in the consciousness of God's love, that He knows me by name, and watches over me in the open and secret places.

Love: The Formula for Winning Spiritual Warfare

Many of us need not fight the spiritual and physical battles we fight today in our homes, relationships, or at our various workplaces, if we allow the Holy Spirit to work out His love in our hearts. Love is the head of all principalities.

Why? Because the nature of love enlisted in 1 Corinthians 13:1-8 (NKJV), *"Though I speak with the tongues of men and of angels, but have not love, I have become sounding brass or a clanging cymbal. And though I have the gift of prophecy, and understand all mysteries and all knowledge, and though I have all faith, so that I could remove mountains, but have not love, I am nothing. And though I bestow all my goods to feed the poor, and though I give my body to be burned, but have not love, it profits me nothing. Love suffers long and is kind; love does not envy; love does not parade itself, is not puffed up; does not behave rudely, does not seek its own, is not provoked, thinks no evil; does not rejoice in iniquity, but rejoices in the truth; bears all things, believes all things, hopes all things, endures all things. Love never fails."* This nature of divine love is too hot for the devil to bear. The devil is proud, arrogant by nature, is always in a hurry; he is slanderous, and the epitome of iniquity. But love is humble, rejoices in righteousness, is holy, patient, long-suffering, bears all things, and so on.

If we bring this attitude into every sphere of our lives, our lives will be empowered. The Holy Spirit uses these virtues of love to strengthen our inner person, which enhances our dependency on God to handle people and situations in our lives. This leads us to intercede for situations and people that are unbearable in our lives—bringing healing to our hearts and the lives of others. We are made to understand in 2 Corinthians 10:4-6: *"For the weapons of our warfare are not carnal but mighty in God for pulling down strongholds, casting down arguments and every high thing that exalts itself against the knowledge of God, bringing every thought into captivity to the obedience of Christ, and being ready to punish all disobedience when your obedience is fulfilled."*

We must learn to cast out every evil thought and pray for those whom we think are our problems—wherever we find ourselves. No matter how unbearable people or situations are, if we refuse bitterness in our hearts and forgive as Christ said we should forgive our offenders, intercede and pray for the help of God who knows how to reward everyone according to their deeds. Then God will punish all disobedience when we have fulfilled all obedience of the nature of love in our circumstances.

Each day I understand more deeply why Paul the apostle exercised so much concern on the loving nature of his followers that made him say in 1 Corinthians 14:1 that they should make love their highest goal (NLT), and to pursue love (NKJV). That means run and chase after it. We must never give room to hatred and bitterness in our lives—no matter how bad things seem or how we have been treated in the past. God is still God. He still avenges His people; we should not take the law into our own hands. The Bible says it is to God that vengeance belongs (Psalm 94:1), and we just read that until our own obedience is total or fulfilled, disobedience will not be punished. Our love for God makes our enemies God's enemies. If we continually obey and walk in the light of His word, we abide in His love.

God's Love: A Canopy of Protection

Loving God and walking in His love is to daily abide under His canopy of protection. Jesus said that if we obey His commandments, we abide in His love (John 15:10). The commandments of God are born out of His love for humanity. When God gives us a commandment about what to do or what *not* to do, it is for our own good. This is why He allows us free will to choose to obey or disobey, because love does not enforce itself on another's will; but the beloved—out of love—wouldn't want to hurt his or her Lover by doing what the other hates. Everything God does is to protect us; we are His beloved; He knows that our wall of protection is obedience to Him. This is why 1 John 5:18-19 says, *"We know that whoever is born of God does not sin; but he who has been born of God keeps himself, and the wicked one does not touch him. We know that we are of God, and the whole world lies under the sway of the wicked one."* And in 1 John 2:14c: *"Because you are strong, and the word of God abides in you, and you have overcome the wicked one."*

God knows the danger in doing what He says we should

not do. Sin gives us away to the enemy, who will then have a hold on us. This is why he is the accuser of the brethren. We cannot live in sin and abide in God's love. When we live in sin, we are slaves of sin — forfeiting our honourable place in Christ Jesus. This is why Jesus told His disciples in John 8:34-36: *"Most assuredly, I say to you, whoever commits sin is a slave of sin. And a slave does not abide in the house forever, but a son abides forever. Therefore if the Son makes you free, you shall be free indeed."* God wants us to abide forever in the place of protection where the enemy cannot reach us.

I am beginning to have an in-depth understanding of Psalm 91:1-8: *"He who dwells in the secret place of the Most High shall abide under the shadow of the Almighty. I will say of the* L ORD, *'He is my refuge and my fortress; My God, in Him I will trust.' Surely He shall deliver you from the snare of the fowler and from the perilous pestilence. He shall cover you with His feathers, and under His wings you shall take refuge; His truth shall be your shield and buckler. You shall not be afraid of the terror by night, nor of the arrow that flies by day, nor of the pestilence that walks in darkness, nor of the destruction that lays waste at noonday. A thousand may fall at your side, and ten thousand at your right hand; but it shall not come near you. Only with your eyes shall you look, and see the reward of the wicked."* To dwell in the secret place of the Most High is to continually abide in His love. This is why it is only those that break the hedge that the serpent will bite. Verses 14-16 of Psalm 91 read: *"Because he has set his love upon Me, therefore I will deliver him; I will set him on high, because he has known My name. He shall call upon Me, and I will answer him; I will be with him in trouble; I will deliver him and honor him. With long life I will satisfy him, and show him My salvation."* Amen.

The blood of Jesus is the blood of His love; this is why the blood protects. Beyond the covenant, love is what sustains the covenant. People break covenants with God because of selfish motives in entering the covenants in the first place; but God remains faithful. No wonder that Jesus said those whom the Father has given to Him no one can snatch from the hand of the Father (John 10:28). Alleluia! Our lives are hidden in Christ and Christ in God. Amen.

Love: The Pathway to Internal Freedom and Magnanimity

The extent to which we live and walk in God's love is the extent to which we experience inner freedom to become all we are created to be and to be true to ourselves. We don't have to pretend to be someone else, or hide under the shadow of someone else, to feel important in life. This in turn helps us to see other people as deserving to be free to be who they really are — without attempting to manipulate them to be like us, or to criticise them for being themselves. Nobody wants to relate with someone who treats him or her as things and not as human beings; everyone wants to be free to express himself or herself: to love and be loved, to respect others and be respected. Everyone wants to be understood. All these we can be to people if we allow the power at work in us — the very life of Jesus in us — to be worked out by the Holy Spirit.

The problem with most of us is that we have not experienced real love in life, so it becomes impossible to love others. Maybe we grew up in a hostile environment, and that has become the lens through which we see life. Irrespective of the environment we were brought up in, the unloving parents we might have, and the low self-esteem we might feel in our hearts, they are not the true reflections of who we really are and how lovable we are. We read from Ephesians 3:14-20 about the depth of God's love for us and its implications in our lives: *"For this reason I bow my knees to the Father of our Lord Jesus Christ, from whom the whole family in heaven and earth is named, that He would grant you, according to the riches of His glory, to be strengthened with might through His Spirit in the inner man, that Christ may dwell in your hearts through faith; that you, being rooted and grounded in love, may be able to comprehend with all the saints what is the width and length and depth and height – to know the love of Christ which passes knowledge; that you may be filled with all the fullness of God.*

Now to Him who is able to do exceedingly abundantly above all that we ask or think, according to the power that works in us."

Who we are in God is what matters. It doesn't matter whether our parents think we came into the world accidentally or by chance, but from the foundation of the world we were in God's plan. This we know from Ephesians 2:10: *"For we are His workmanship, created in Christ Jesus for good works, which God prepared beforehand that we should walk in them."* From here we see that no one was ever an accident; we were all in God's agenda at creation. Understanding this depth of God's heart and purpose for us should establish us in His love and set us free to live our best life. Even when it seems no one cares, God says He will never leave nor forsake us (Hebrews 13:5).

The Bible teaches us in 2 Corinthians 3:18: *"But we all, with unveiled face, beholding as in a mirror the glory of the Lord, are being transformed into the same image from glory to glory, just as by the Spirit of the Lord."* The only Person Who has the final say about who we are is God, and this we know; that we were made in His image and likeness. We just read that the more we behold, as in a mirror, the glory of God, that we too are changed from glory to glory.

Chapter Five

The word of God is the mirror of God because in John 1:1 we read that *"In the beginning was the Word, and the Word was with God, and the Word was God."* If we spend time in God's word, we will find out who we are in Him and how much He loves us. The more of God we know, the more of ourselves we discover. This will destroy low self-esteem, inferiority complexes, and the inability to love. On the other hand, we will increase our capacity to love others and ourselves in return.

Oftentimes, I see people who seem to be extremely quiet and keep to themselves. Everyone accepts them as being quiet, but when I get close to them and show them that they are accepted and loved as they are, they suddenly become relaxed and begin to relate differently and become vocal. As I continually interact with them, I discover that a good number of them have hidden pain and inner struggles resulting from their past experiences. These memories are bottled up in their hearts, keeping them from enjoying their present lives. I talk with them about their inner struggles, encouraging them to face those issues one by one. Eventually, they let go of the past and allowed their inner spirits free to face the present and build their futures. Over time, as they yielded to my counsel and allowed God into their lives, they experienced tremendous healings, became free to relate without fear or suspicion, and are happy people today.

On the other hand, I have met people who seemed like extroverts. They smiled at everybody and wanted approval from everybody. I discovered that only a few of these people have found genuine freedom in their inner person. They want it but are acting it out without going through the real process. This brings about frustration, anger, and pain when their expectations of approval are not met. These people are searching for love and acceptance in the wrong places. They need to find themselves first to know who they are in God. Until a man or a woman loves himself or herself enough, he or she will live their lives seeking to be loved and approved of. It takes self-discovery, acceptance, and assertiveness in God to be rooted and have firm foundations to build our lives on.

Love brings about freedom of the inner person. The Bible says in 2 Corinthians 3:17: *"Now the Lord is the Spirit; and where the Spirit of the Lord is, there is liberty."* When we are in the love of God, we are free to soar, to love and be loved, and to share with others the river of God's life in us; but it takes the process of finding ourselves in God and God in us, allowing God to work through and in us. To break the hardness of our hearts to give us a heart of flesh, this process might be painful. We might have to learn the hard way through rejections from people, disappointments from loved ones, and abandonment by those we expect to love us. If we fall into the hands of God, He will turn what the enemy meant for evil into good, set us free from the limitations of humankind, and connect us to His limitlessness — enabling us to live a life of magnanimity above pettiness and breaking every boundary to becoming our best in God.

I am a living testimony of how God can work in the hearts of His children. As a child, I was loved and loving, but growing up, the enemy planted an evil seed in my life for me to begin to experience hatred and rejection. This brought upon me all manner of emotional trauma. From primary school to university, people hated me for no reason. I was slandered and falsely accused of many things I knew nothing about, which led to breakdowns of relationships I cherished. It made life unbearable — to the point of suicidal thoughts. I remember vividly an episode of my life that occurred in May 2006. It was a shameful situation in which I lost a relationship to lies and slander. In return, I was badly assaulted verbally by the very one who claimed to love and cherish me in secret. In the midst of that suffering and rejection, I found a place of forgiveness in my heart for the very ones who had treated me wrongly. Without waiting for them to apologise, I rested my case in heaven's court. As I did that, God helped me to overcome the devil; He restored my reputation without me feeling malice or holding grudges against any of my offenders. I knew the great and colourful destiny ahead of me; I was quick to know, through various great authors I have met through books, that the enemy always fights to destroy great destinies. So, I took my stand with whom God says I am. He helped me to be magnanimous in that situation and healed my broken heart and life. Today, I am whole and able to love those same people at no cost.

I also discovered that when people hurt me, I don't let go of them easily because of my attachment to them. I continually shower them with phone calls, irrespective of their responses. I buy them gifts, books especially. Before I know it, the hurt is gone, and I forget them and all the wrongs they ever did to me. It was my own healing therapy — and it did work for me because I have always been scared of hating anyone. I am very sure that if some of those people are reading this book, they will testify to this.

In the year 2001, I read *The Final Quest* by Rick Joyner. I was using public transport from Lagos to Ibadan, Nigeria. I reached a point in the book where I broke down in tears. The vision written in the book concerned what I was going through at that time — slander and rejection. The person sitting next to me had no clue what was happening to me, but my God and I knew. At that point, the reality of who I am in God became clear to me; it hit me that I was not an ordinary person. The devil was out to upstage me, so I developed more doses of love in my heart. Love helped me survive events and circumstances that would have made me give up on life; in the process, I became my own best friend until I found Jesus; then He made life more beautiful.

Give God a chance to teach, nurse, and nurture you in this greatest spiritual gift; you will love life more and enjoy it more.

God's Love: A Pathway to Accelerated Spiritual Growth

I have discovered that the easiest route to spiritual growth is to have the heart of a child, to love and live like a child. No wonder Jesus told His disciples in Mark 10:15, *"Assuredly, I say to you, whoever does not receive the kingdom of God as a little child will by no means enter it."* Jesus was referring to the state of our hearts; it takes a pure heart of love to believe all things. The Bible says the pure in heart shall see God (Matthew 5:8); this is the state of the heart of a child, innocent and devoid of the knowledge of the evil in the world.

This is why children don't take offenses seriously. No matter what you do to them, they forgive easily and still remain your friends. These actions may make some people suspicious. They might reject our expressions of love or acts of kindness, or even misunderstand what we stand for. In all of these situations, the Holy Spirit is able to work quickly in our lives by using those rejections, misunderstandings, and offenses to build us up—helping us to achieve balance in our love ministry. To know when to hold back and watch, or to continue showing love to people depends on the circumstances at hand. The Holy Spirit will always be there to direct us in what to do.

The truth is that there are people who take kindness and

expressions of love to mean stupidity or acts of weakness. They might want to take advantage of them, but the Holy Spirit restrains them and helps to expose such people. With time, it becomes easy to recognize such people when we meet them. And if you look closely at such people's lives, they are "lone rangers"; yet they think they are the smartest. They know how to use people and dump them; but for the person who walks in love, God always exposes manipulative people.

Living and walking in love is living and walking in God. The more we walk in love, the more spiritual height we gain.

Walking in God's Love is to Daily Walk in His Wisdom

When we walk in the love of God, we walk in His wisdom. The Bible says Jesus Christ is the wisdom and power of God (1 Corinthians 1:18). As we abide in Him, He makes His counsel available to us each time. The Bible says the secret of the Lord is with them that fear Him (Malachi 2:5). Loving Him puts us at a place of reverence for Him. This qualifies us and gives us access to His wisdom daily. Amen.

Love: The Road to Unity and Success

The most powerful people on earth aren't really the people living in affluence or in a high position. You may wonder why. Money has wings and does fly away; earthly positions are temporal. The Bible testifies that we can give to people without love, which will only produce temporary associations for as long as the other person is dependent on us; but the moment they gain their independence, we lose relevance in their lives. It's the same with positions; once a person is no longer in a position of authority, he or she loses relevance to those who were once hovering around them.

The most powerful people on earth are those with the greatest capacity to love because they are the instruments of change, and representatives of God on earth. They understand the heart and the language of God in relating with humankind, His creatures. They are people who have hung around God enough, and submitted themselves to be humbled enough, to enlarge their capacity to become nothing while God becomes all—Humility personified. Jesus is a perfect example. He related with and brought people together in spite of their differences. This bond of unity he created in His lifetime ministry became one of His last prayers for His church before His departure; that there should be oneness in the body (John 17:21-23).

Unity is a strong force to reckon with on the path to achieving any goal in life. This reminds me of a Christian movie I watched, titled *Joshua*. It is about a young man who came into a community where there was no love; no one cared about others. His mission was to teach the people love and understanding, it doesn't matter who the people were; he related with them and always brought himself to the level of the people and rendered assistance to them when they needed it. He brought the people in the community together. They even rebuilt the abandoned, thunderstorm-wrecked community church. The lives of the people changed; they learnt to love one another, to share, and to spend time together.

People became so endeared to Joshua—who was neither a pastor nor any leader of any sort—that he became a threat to the religious leaders in the community. His word became authority, not out of compulsion or force, but a spontaneous response to love. This is what we all can become; in turn, we can experience tremendous success as a boss, a manager, a team leader, or a member of a community. From the above story, we see the word of Jesus Christ come to bear when He told His disciples that those who want to be great in the kingdom of God must become servants (Matthew 20:26). Service to God and humankind is the route to greatness in God's kingdom. Joshua in the above story was nothing in his own eyes; he humbled himself and was able to understand the men and women of the community. Love gives room for people to be themselves and to express themselves. In the process, we are able to know more about people, cities, and nations. These, I believe, were the secrets of Joshua: simplicity of heart, humility, and understanding. In the end, he became indispensable and a strong force to reckon with.

Love heals and delivers. I believe it was the love in the heart of our Lord Jesus Christ that made His ministry on earth a success.

Love: Eternity on Course and Eternity Secured

We read in Luke 10:25-37 the story of the lawyer who came to Jesus, asking what to do to inherit eternal life. Jesus asked him what he read from the law, and he said in verse 27: *"You shall love the LORD your God with all your heart, with all your soul, with all your strength, and with all your mind, and your neighbour as yourself."* Jesus told him to go and do as he has just said, and he shall live; but the lawyer went further and asked Jesus who his neighbour was. Jesus told him the parable of the Good Samaritan from verses 30-37: *"A certain man went down from Jerusalem to Jericho, and fell among thieves, who stripped him of his clothing, wounded him, and departed, leaving him half dead. Now by chance a certain priest came down that road. And when he saw him, he passed by on the other side. Likewise a Levite, when he arrived at the place, came and looked, and passed by on the other side. But a certain Samaritan, as he journeyed, came where he was. And when he saw him, he had compassion. So he went to him and bandaged his wounds, pouring on oil and wine; and he set him on his own animal, brought him to an inn, and took care of him. On the next day, when he departed, he took out two denarii, gave them to the innkeeper, and said to him, 'Take care of him; and whatever more you spend, when I come again, I will repay you.' "So which of these three do you think was neighbour to him who fell among the thieves?" And he said, "He who showed mercy on him." Then Jesus said to him, "Go and do likewise."*

From the above scripture, Jesus expounded more on the greatest commandment and what is expected of us in loving our fellow human beings. It becomes clear what 1 John 4:17 means by being perfected in love so that we might be bold on Judgment Day. The lawyer only asked Jesus what it entails to inherit eternal life, and it was summarized with the compassion of the Good Samaritan. We note here that Jesus focused neither on the priest nor the Levite but on the Samaritan because of his heart of compassion—which is love in action. There is a reason why Jesus illustrates this to us: to let us know the core issues in the heart of the Father, and to let us know that even the unbelievers are important to God because He created them and has purchased their redemption by the blood of His Son, Jesus.

Eternity and God's love are inseparable. Jesus promised eternal life to those who believe in Him. Eternal life is the God kind of life; it is timeless and of immense quality. It is called the Zoe kind of life. When we walk in the light of the love of God, we display and manifest the life of God that is in us. That is why the scripture says, *"as He is, so are we in this world."* Everything about us—the way we live, act, think, talk, and dress—must reflect Christ. Walking in His steps of righteousness and love helps us in the fulfillment of the law. This is our only assurance of boldness on the Day of Judgment. Amen.

Implications of a Closed Heart

Those who have chosen to close their hearts to the love of God and to others usually have very frustrating lives; they are usually myopic, judgmental, and suspicious of people. They use others to achieve their goals without caring about them — as long as they themselves are okay. They are people who find their way to the top by manipulation and intimidation, irrespective of who gets hurt in the process. And when they get there, the top is singularly for them.

A closed heart is a closed destiny. The Bible says that out of the heart flows the issue of life (Proverbs 4:23). Nothing can flow into a closed heart from God and out of it to others. It is like a dead, stagnant, and motionless sea. A person who cannot be moved or touched by others will not be able to reach out to someone else. It only leads to a life of frustration. Such people should be encouraged and counselled to open their hearts to the wonderful life that God has given to us.

I know a fifty-year-old man who lives such a life. No matter what you tell him, he doesn't seem to see anything wrong with it. He doesn't interact with people much, but he is always officious. He has lived alone since I have known him; he has never married. I have never seen him hang around anyone, such as close friends or family, but careerwise he is doing well. I actually got close to him in spite of the fact that people see him as an impossible person. As I got closer to him, I found a man who has internal struggles and is afraid of rejection. I never had the opportunity to know his past, but I sure know that there are reasons for his chosen lifestyle. Though he is deceiving himself that he is not a lonely person, I can tell that he returned my love and regard because of my way of relating with him. Even though initially he resisted allowing me close to him, all he needed was to be convinced that I was harmless. Yet in my private corner, I prayed for his liberation, even though he thinks all is well. What amazes me is that he is a Christian.

WHAT TO DO:
1. Open your heart to the love of God.
2. Accept it.
3. Study the word of God; soak yourself in it through meditation.
4. Have fellowship time with God—privately and in church.
5. Have fellowship with others.
6. Search your heart for any bitterness. Forgive and forget the past.
7. Ask God to help you let go of the past.
8. Invite the Holy Spirit to teach you how to show love to others.
9. Be thankful to God and sing worship songs to Him and to yourself.
10. Listen to inspirational Christian songs.
11. Consciously reach out to people in the church. Maintain a good church life and good relationships with other brothers and sisters.
12. Give yourself and what you have to God; also have a willing heart to help others when you are in the position to help.

The devil knows the power in loving and being loved. It is all we need in the world today to heal our broken dreams, decayed society, wayward children and loved ones, wars, hatred for one another, and religious and communal clashes.

If we really love God, we will not kill one another for any reason. No person who loves and values his or her life will destroy another life. The love of God is the answer to our coldheartedness and infectious greed. If we open our hearts to the love of God, we will see the possibilities and reasons to overcome our fears, compulsions, and inner struggles.

If we love one another, we will look out for the welfare of one another. Compulsively accumulating wealth while other people are suffering will be untold of us; we are blessed to be a blessing. It takes a heart attuned with God to give to those in need. The Bible makes us understand that the worth of a person is not in his or her possessions.

How Do We Bring God's Love Into Our Relationships?

In our day-to-day relationships from our homes, to school, offices and public places, we have to be conscious of God's presence with us. Wherever God is, love thrives.

In 1 Corinthians 13:1-8, as we read before, Paul the apostle made us understand that the greatest spiritual gift is love. In verse 13, he concluded: *"and now abide faith, hope, love, these three; but the greatest of these is love."*

From the above scripture, we see that love is the greatest of all; the nature of love is the holy nature of God. We see that everything we do in life must be motivated by love for it to be real and be of any impact. It is amazing to note that even charity not motivated by love has no reward. Out of necessity, we must strive to bring this aspect of God's love into our relationships—bearing with one another and correcting one another in love. This chapter of the Bible is worth a lifetime of meditation and practise. Therefore, we should try as much as we can to:

1. Treat everyone we meet equally; no matter his or her status.
2. To render help to those in need — if within our means.
3. If anyone is nasty and rude, we should correct him or her in love in order for our light to shine.
4. To never give room to lust or iniquity in our hearts because love and lust do not cohabit. Love is holy and rejoices in truth.

Chapter Six

Manifesting God's Love in Our Relationships

"However nothing is more important in a believer's consecration than his love. Whether his consecration is true or false depend upon whether or not there is consecration of love. Love is the touchstone of consecration." —Watchman Nee

In the world today, we are experiencing a lot of challenges in our relationships; that is, casual or close friendships, courtships, and marriages. So many Christian marriages are crumbling due to the foundation on which it was built. The Bible makes us understand that *"if the foundations are destroyed, what can the righteous do?"* (Psalm 11:3). If love is a spirit, then any relationship built on the soul's realm based on emotions and feelings cannot survive the test of time. Only that which emanates from the Spirit of God is real and can survive the test of time.

No one has the capacity to truly love—except by the power of the Holy Spirit. As children of God, when we allow the Holy Spirit to help us grow in the love of God, it overflows to those around us; we begin to think and behave like God. To operate from the love realm is to become supernatural beings; it is a realm of the celestials, of men and women who have allowed God to perform the work of the cross in their hearts, as discussed in the previous chapter. The flesh no longer has a hold on them.

Using Jesus as our example, you will agree with me that while He walked on earth, He had relationships with His disciples and other people. We read about His relationships with the two sisters Martha and Mary, their brother Lazarus, and Mary Magdalene; yet there was no documented scandal of Jesus in fornication, confusion, instability, lying, cheating, or manipulating others. He lived without sin. We read of accounts when men in biblical times came to put Him in tight corners and asked Him questions that they thought would catch Him unawares; yet He was consistent in His word because He is Love and Truth personified.

As Christians, Jesus should be our example in every relationship we keep — whether with casual friends at our places of work, believers or unbelievers alike, or with close relations — our words and conduct must glorify God. If we are going to influence our generation for Jesus, we must learn to be "love dynamite" for God; not in a worldly sense, but in absolute obedience to God's word. For example, 1 John 2:15-17 says, *"We should not love the world or the things that are in the world. If anyone loves the world, the love of the Father is not in Him. For all that is in the world – the lust of the flesh, the lust of the eyes, and the pride of life – is not of the Father, but of the world. And the world is passing away, and the lust of it; but he who does the will of God abides forever."*

We cannot be called the light of the world and still be doing and saying what people in darkness do and say. Why on earth would they listen to us? The Bible says "…they speak as of the world because they are of the world" (1 John 4:5). My beloved brothers and sisters, to effectively fulfill our divine mandate of soul winning with our lifestyle, we must learn how to keep our relationships with one another — and those with the people of the world — godly and pure.

I always tell my friends that it's not that I have stopped

being a human being with feelings; and with the help of the Holy Spirit, I have been able to grasp God's perspective of love. This has helped me to see divinity in everyone I come in contact with. God, by His mercy and grace, has helped me to relate to them as though God sent them my way in that moment to represent Him. Jesus said in Mark 9:37, *"Whoever receives one of these little children in My name receives Me; and whoever receives Me, receives not Me but Him who sent Me."* God has given us a great task; we need understanding, grace, and humility to fulfill this task of love and acceptance of people in the name of God. It's not because of who the people are, but because of the God in whose image they were created. God is in us all.

We must come to terms with the truth that feelings and emotions cannot be stable if the Spirit of love does not power them. The soul of a person, the seat of emotions and feelings, is subject to change by circumstances. But for the spiritual person, the Spirit is in charge — putting the soul under subjection to the scrutiny of the word of God; this is what stabilises feelings and emotions to cultivate godly relationships and to be instruments of righteousness in the hand of God.

It is a conscious choice to love God's way and not the way of the world. I have met men and women who told me I have radically changed their perception of love. One of those people motivated me to put this message in writing.

The devil knows the power of loving people just as God loves them. That is why he has released the spirits of lust and hatred in the world, making people grow cold and selfish towards one another. Also, he makes it seem as if it is impossible for the church of God to be one as Christ desired it to be; for believers to work or do business together without cheating one another, or being jealous or envious of one another; or for two young believers of the opposite sex to be good friends without becoming lustful towards each other. Should that happen, they begin to use language such as "they are falling in love."

The people of the world are not regenerated in their inner selves; they cannot exhibit the above features because of the fallen state of humankind. They can fall in and out of love, but we in the kingdom of God are to be perpetually in the state of love because the Spirit of God — the Spirit of Love — resides in us.

The Holy Spirit needs our consent to work this love of God in us. If we are determined to follow the path of our Lord Jesus Christ, then our hearts must be opened. We must always remember what the Bible says: that narrow and difficult is the road that leads to life (Matthew 7:14). Jesus is that Way, and His language is the language of love. This is why it's important that our opened hearts are filled with the word of God; this will help build a healthy discernment in us because the Spirit behind the Word will serve as a searchlight, guiding and helping us through every relationship or person we come in contact with.

When light shines in darkness, darkness always bows; that light is Jesus Christ, and He is the epitome of love. This is why love never fails. The only way we can manifest the love of God in our relationships is to display godly virtues.

There are other kinds of relationships where we find ourselves outside our relationship with the Lord. They are:
1. Family members.
2. Unbelievers around us.
3. Friends.
4. The marital relationship.

Chapter Six

Working Out Godly Relationships in Our Families

When I refer to family members, I mean both our physical and spiritual family members. Our physical family members are our biological parents and siblings, and our spiritual family is our relationship as a member of God's family; that is, members of our local assembly and other Christians. Jesus said in Matthew 12:50: *"For whoever does the will of My Father in heaven is My brother and sister and mother."* In the light of this scripture, He made us understand that we should have close ties with our brothers and sisters in the faith in order to be on course with the Lord.

If our biological family members are not of the household of God, they might uphold cultures and traditions that contradict the word of God and will make us sin against God. We must learn to respectfully let them know our faith and why we cannot follow those cultures and traditions. Meanwhile, we will pray for them in our secret corners for God to grant them salvation and understanding of His ways.

We must honour and respect our earthly and spiritual parents and walk in love with our brothers and sisters. But in situations where our parents and relatives are not of the faith, we are not to give in to any doctrine that contradicts the word of God. The Bible says, "[O]bey your parents in the Lord" (Ephesians 6:1). This is a very key issue. I have seen and heard of believers dragged into doing wrong things due to pressure from unbelieving parents; this puts the believer in perpetual bondage and rebellion against God.

If you are going through any such problems, seek the face of God for a change of heart for them and that the light of the gospel will shine in their hearts to receive Jesus as their Lord and Savior — and come to the knowledge of God.

More so, as a member of the household of God, we must

have harmonious relationships and be friendly towards one another. It hurts me to see brethren defrauding, lying to, and defiling one another. These sins should not be named among us as children of light. Righteousness and justice are the foundations of the throne of God. These must be our foundation as His children.

The foundation upon which a family stands determines the kind of relationships they will have with others, whether godly or ungodly. For example, if a child is from a home where the love and fear of God are exalted, such a child will grow up with the love and the fear of God. A lot of parents themselves do not even know what it means to love; maybe they did not experience it themselves growing up; perhaps they grew up with hostile parents or relatives. Along the line, they found Jesus; yet they maintain their own ideas of what it means to bring up a child according to their own experiences and not by the word of God. This is why we find homes where parents are believers; they are spirit filled and speaking in tongues. However, they are talking but are not enjoying harmonious relationships as couples; the husband does what he likes—and likewise the wife—while the children are watching the drama in the home.

These kinds of attitudes that parents exhibit send signals to the children in their hearts as they grow up. The consequences of this will be: raising daughters who are broken, desperately in search of love and comfort, which subjects them to all manner of peer and societal pressure. Sons will find it easy to lie and commit atrocities without looking back at possible damages to their lives and those of others. Our youths are broken, confused, and suffer from low self-esteem. They are being abused day in and day out because fathers and mothers have refused to take their rightful places.

We read in Genesis 34:1-4, the story of Dinah, Jacob's

daughter. The Bible says, *"Now Dinah the daughter of Leah, whom she had borne to Jacob, went out to see the daughters of the land. And when Shechem the son of Hamor the Hivite, prince of the country, saw her, he took her and lay with her, and violated her. His soul was strongly attracted to Dinah the daughter of Jacob, and he loved the young woman and spoke kindly to the young woman. So Shechem spoke to his father Hamor, saying, 'Get me this young woman as a wife.'"*

We all know the story of Jacob and her mother Leah; there was no affection between them because her father was in love with Rachel, her stepmother. This placed her mother in a disadvantaged position, making her seek the love of her husband instead of looking after the children. I believe Dinah was alone at home; she needed someone to talk to, and that pushed her out of the house to see the daughters of the land. After all, she is the only young lady we read about in the Bible in which "daughter" was used. In the process, she was violated and defiled by a man who had desired her secretly in his heart. This singular episode was a devastating one—not only for her, but for her entire family and the community. There was shedding of innocent blood, as indicated in Genesis 34:27: *"The sons of Jacob came upon the slain, and plundered the city, because their sister had been defiled."* At the end of Jacob's life, while prophesying over his children, he was still mindful of what transpired in Shechem, placing a curse on Simeon and Levi. Read Genesis 49:5-7 with me, *"Simeon and Levi are brothers; Instruments of cruelty are in their dwelling place. Let not my soul enter their council; Let not my honor be united to their assembly; For in their anger they slew a man, and in their self-will they hamstrung an ox. Cursed be their anger, for it is fierce; and their wrath, for it is cruel! I will divide them in Jacob and scatter them in Israel."* This is an implication of a home built on a faulty foundation; it brings about generational problems that require only the mercy of God to resolve.

This is why the Bible says train up a child in the way that he should go (Proverbs 22:6), so that when he or she grows up, the child will not depart from it. Where have our fathers and mothers gone? What have they learnt of God and life to pass on to us to live right? Are their egos, self-pride, respect, and ambition more important to them than their ministry of love and care in the home?

This book would not be complete in discussing working out godly relationships without mentioning the parents. What becomes of a child who grows up watching his or her father tell lies or act unrighteously? I sincerely believe that parents are God's representatives here on earth to ensure that the virtue of love God has endowed us with does not die. Parents must be role models of love and care to their children and their neighbours. My appeal to parents is to be examples of Christ to their children and those around them.

Working Out Godly Relationships With Unbelievers

For the unbelievers around us, the Bible enjoins us in 2 Corinthians 6:14: *"Do not be unequally yoked together with unbelievers. For what fellowship has righteousness with lawlessness? And what communion is light with darkness?"* As children of God wanting to keep godly relationships, unbelievers are not the kind of friends we can have close ties with because righteousness and lawlessness cannot work together, and evil communication corrupts good manners.

When we keep unbelieving friends close to us, they will pollute our walk with God. We owe them our love and can relate to them to serve as an example for them to see.

However, we should not be in their company, spending so much time with them and involving ourselves in ungodly discussions. It is very detrimental to our Christian walk, depending on our level of maturity. For a babe in Christ, it is advisable to keep your distance; but for a mature Christian grounded in the word of God, our aim should be to win their souls to God by our lifestyle, counsel, and testimonies.

I remember when I was living with an unbelieving family. I clearly saw the difference in their words and mine. Most times the topics of discussion so nauseated me that I excused myself and went to my room. I have had times when they would come to me for counsel on a matter that is sinful. After giving my candid counsel, they would tell me: "That one is for you oh, because body no be wood." So, you can imagine that staying in such an environment for long will have negative side effects on our walk with God.

On a certain morning, I was reading my Bible. One of the ladies came into my room. Despite the fact that she saw me with my Bible open in my hands, she started discussing her sexual relationship with her boyfriend. Can you see how keeping close ties with unbelievers can drag us to sin? I had to run for my life by relocating to somewhere else.

1 Peter 2:11-12 says: *"Beloved, I beg you as sojourners and pilgrims, abstain from fleshly lusts which war against the soul, having your conduct honourable among the Gentiles, that when they speak against you as evildoers, they may by your good works which they observe, glorify God in the day of visitation."* With this scripture, we see that our lifestyle is very important when we have unbelievers around us. It will help draw them to the kingdom as they see the differences between our lives and theirs.

God implores us to love our neighbour as ourselves, unbelievers inclusive. When they need our help and love, we must show it to them; that is what we owe them.

The Bible enjoins us in Colossians 4:5 *"to walk in wisdom with those who are outside, redeeming the time."* This is because we are in evil days, as indicated in Ephesians 5:16. We must have it in the back of our minds that our value system as Christians is different from that of unbelievers. Whenever we relate with them, we relate in wisdom in order to avoid unnecessary strife and arguments. If at all, our focus should be on how we can reach them with the love of Christ through our prayers, lifestyle, and compassion towards them in order for them to see the light and come to the saving knowledge of our Lord Jesus Christ.

Working Out Godly Relationships in Friendship

Quite some time ago, the Holy Spirit ministered to me that friendship is a must-do class in the school of the Spirit that God uses to work many things into our lives. These include: tolerance, endurance, and celebration of others—irrespective of who they are and whatever they do or might have done to hurt us. It is a required route to physical, emotional, and spiritual maturity.

So many people are finding it difficult to keep healthy friendships because of the evil in the world today. We are not of the world and shouldn't have the problems or fears that the people of the world have. The problem with most of us, especially young people, is our spiritual laziness and the worldly standards we have set for ourselves. If as young people we give our hearts to God and allow the power of the Holy Spirit to work in us, guiding and directing our lives, we will not have problems developing healthy — — — friendships in school, at work, or in church. Like begets like; if we know Who God is, we will know who a child of God is when we come in contact with one.

And when we come in contact with someone who claims to be a child of God but his or her lifestyle does not reflect it, the Bible is very clear about it in 1 Corinthians 5:9-11: *"I wrote to you in my epistle not to keep company with sexually immoral people. Yet I certainly did not mean with the sexually immoral people of this world, or with the covetous, or extortioners, or idolaters, since then you would need to go out of the world. But now I have written to you not to keep company with anyone named a brother, who is sexually immoral, or covetous, or an idolater, or a reviler, or a drunkard, or an extortioner – not even to eat with such a person."*

If a believing brother or sister does not exalt righteousness, we must correct them in truth and love; if they refuse to change, we should leave them alone while we continually pray that God would touch their hearts and change them. But we should not hang around them as close friends, because evil communication corrupts good manners.

Friendship with the Opposite Sex

In the church today, believers struggle with how to keep godly relationships with the opposite sex without strings attached. I have often heard in Christian gatherings the discouragement of friendship with the opposite sex until the person is ready for marriage. Friendship is an integral part of human relationships irrespective of gender; the most important thing is the foundation on which it is built. The Bible says to teach children in the way they should go, and they will not depart from it when they grow up (Proverbs 22:6). We cannot afford to allow our youths to grow frail without strength to resist temptation—making it impossible for them to survive the outside world when they are on their own.

The Bible says in Colossians 2:20-23 (NLT), *"You have died with Christ, and he has set you free from the spiritual powers of this world. So why do you keep on following the rules of the world, such as, "Don't handle! Don't taste! Don't touch!"? Such rules are mere human teachings about things that deteriorate as we use them. These rules may seem wise because they require strong devotion, pious self-denial, and severe bodily discipline. But they provide no help in conquering a person's evil desire."* I love the way the New King James Version puts the last verse of this scripture; it says in Colossians 2:23 (NKJV): *"These things indeed have an appearance of wisdom in self-imposed religion, false humility, and neglect of the body, but are of no value against the indulgence of the flesh."*

"[They] are of no value against the indulgence of the flesh." When we set rules and regulations of what and what not to do, they are good; but they are of little value in dealing with the indulgence of the flesh. But there are ways in which we can come to the knowledge of the truth to dwell in the love of God — through understanding and the impartation of His Spirit that the flesh is dealt with by the Spirit of God. If it is not dealt with from the Spirit, rules and regulations will always fail us because we are trying to do things by our own strength. As a young single lady, over the years, God has taught me and shown me that He desires His children to relate with one another in order to profit one another without violating His commandments.

There is nothing wrong with being friends with the opposite sex, but the foundation of the individuals is important and the stage of growth and development they have attained in God. Individual understanding of self is very important in such relationships.

Friendship with the opposite sex could be casual, close, or intimate; but ultimately, it is that the friendship should be pure. A casual friend is an acquaintance that we are yet to know very well; we meet them in church or at work. A close friend is someone we have common interests with, and oftentimes we like to talk about those things we have in common. An intimate friend is someone we share our dreams and personal experiences with in order to counsel one another. The Bible makes us understand the essence of friendship. Proverbs 18:24 says, *"A man who has friends must himself be friendly, but there is a friend who sticks closer than a brother."* Read Proverbs 27:17: *"As iron sharpens iron, so a man sharpens the countenance of his friend."* And Proverbs 27:6 says, *"Faithful are the wounds of a friend, but the kisses of an enemy are deceitful."*

We read from the above scriptures that the essence of friendship is to be able to sharpen one another in correction, in sharing of knowledge, and in unity of purpose.

Why Is There So Much Confusion In Opposite-Sex Friendship?

So much confusion and problems exist because most people have yet to discover their purpose in life. So, they focus on the mundane things. This makes it difficult for them to define their relationships when they meet new people.

Purpose is very important to everything we do in life; if we have not been able to identify our talents and gifts, our scope for everything — including friendship — will be limited. Dr Myles Munroe said, "When purpose is not known, abuse is inevitable." A man or woman of purpose is a conscious, dangerous person. Why? Because everything he or she does is with a purpose.

When young men and ladies are trained to operate and run their lives from the pivot of purpose, the people they meet on their way in life will make more sense to them than they presently do. For me, when I meet someone of the opposite sex who is a believer, nothing romantic comes to mind; God has brought another brother my way. If we have a common ground to relate in, such as a common vision, I keep such people as my friends—in the pure sense of friendship, with rules. As time goes on, we know each other better. With time, some friendships naturally fade on their own with no misunderstanding. Life just takes care of them after these men have fulfilled their mission and what they are to impart in my life. There will still be one or two who, through the years, are still my friends. They have become more like family.

I understand that there are situations where, in the process of building friendship, one of the parties starts developing an emotional attachment to the other. In all sincerity, I tell every lady I counsel that no matter how interesting they find their male friends, they are not permitted to be emotionally attached to a man who has yet to propose marriage to them. This is where emotional maturity comes in. This also applies to the guys.

Emotional maturity is important in friendship because it helps us to keep our emotions in check and under control. I remember one of the singles meetings we had some time back. During the question-and-answer session, people asked about topics you would never expect to come from believers' mouths—or should even exist in their minds. The moderator, with an expression of irritation on her face, stood up upset and said, "What is wrong with you, these children? Where is the Holy Spirit in your life?" I felt what she felt, because from the questions asked, I perceived these youths were struggling with their sexuality and understanding of love in relating with one another.

Chapter Six

Practical Steps to Keeping Godly Friendships with the Opposite Sex

Oftentimes, people argue about the practicality of keeping godly friendships that last. Just as anything one does without faith is sin, so is a friendship we try to build by ourselves. It is only the friendship breathed upon by the Holy Spirit that lasts and yields fruit. The essence is for unity of purpose to further the kingdom of God.

I sincerely believe that young people should be taught to allow God to take over all their affairs —

including choosing their friends. Throughout my Christian journey, I have never chosen any friend for myself, whether it is the same or opposite sex. The Lord taught me how spiritually dangerous it is to have the wrong person as a friend; he or she could serve as a loophole for the enemy in a person's life.

If we commit our hearts to the Holy Spirit and His training of love in our hearts, He will teach us truths and how to apply them in all our relationships. This is an impartation that only He can achieve in our lives. In my own life, the Holy Spirit has imparted the truths below to me; they have helped me constantly in my relationships with others — especially in the secret thoughts of my heart.

He said that there are two voices that constantly whisper to us; the voice of love and the voice of lust. The voice of love is the voice of God, while the voice of lust is the voice of the devil. Love is holy, and therefore has an element of grace in it that helps us to love in a holy way and teaches us to grow in godly love. The end product of love is pleasing God, while that of lust is pleasing the flesh and the devil. How do we bring this practically into our daily dealings with one another?

I found out that we often don't have problems meeting

new people; but we do have problems in sustaining them in purity. The problem in friendship starts when we meet people we have common interests with, that we spend time discussing important issues that we feel we can't do with other people. At that point, we use the word "connect." We tell our friends "we met someone," that we "connected with them so fast it was as if we have known them all our lives." At this point, we feel so happy because we feel within us that at least somebody thinks like us or understands us. It is at this point that the problem usually starts, as either the two parties or one person begins to feel unusually emotional about the friendship, and the voices of love and lust begin to compete for attention.

At this point, the voice of love is ready to train us past the stage of emotions and feelings to be rooted in the genuine love of God; while the voice of lust is ready to destroy that friendship by leading us into sin.

The voice of love encourages the friendship but tells us to cool off our emotions; it is just an excitement that will subside as time goes on, but the voice of lust tells us that we are falling in love. At this point, some ladies or guys begin to tell their friends: "I think I am falling in love with my friend because we can talk for hours on the phone without getting tired, and we are so fond of each other." Children of God don't *fall* in love; we *grow* in love. When you think you are falling in love, check your spiritual life, because carnality is about to set in.

If the emotion that is building up is not understood and brought under the control of the voice of love, which is the voice of God, infatuation comes in, and lust begins to place demands on the flesh. At this immature state of the friendship, they begin to think of taking the friendship to the next level—even when they both know that they are not yet ready for marriage.

Most of them result into the worldly terminology of dating or engaging in a relationship they are not yet ready to handle. Eventually, they fall into the trap of the enemy—lying to each other, and fornicating. This kind of relationship cannot last or stand the test of time—even if both parties end up marrying each other. Problems and possible divorce are inevitable except by the mercies and grace of God because the Spirit of love was not imparted in both parties. The Spirit is the root that enables unconditional love and prepares us for a life of romance.

If both parties hearken to the voice of love, with time those feelings and the excitement will subside. They will be more at ease with themselves and take time to learn more about each other. If it is not a relationship destined to grow into marriage, it will remain at the friendship level God wants it to be. But if it is destined to go beyond friendship, it is wisdom for the man to make his intentions known to the lady and not assume. It is morally wrong for a man to take his close friendship with a lady to automatically mean a marriage relationship. Every believer we meet—whether a guy or a lady—who shares common interests with us, is not accidental, because God is a purposeful God. We cannot afford to forget our heavenly assignment: that we are pilgrims here on earth to bring the kingdom of God down to earth. As children of God, we cannot be myopic in our relationships towards one another. We need one another to do God's work.

When two believers understand what working in unity of purpose for the kingdom of God is, friendship becomes driven by purpose rather than personal emotions. By this understanding love always wins and lust loses.

The note of warning is that at every stage of friendship,

wisdom is required; communications must be kept open and active so that in time the man or the lady knows that both parties are in pure friendship and nothing more. It makes it easier when everything is clear to all, and that there is nothing but friendship.

I met a guy some years ago at a National Prayer Conference. I sat behind him. Somehow, my inner spirit began to communicate with me about him. I didn't know why I wanted to be his friend; unknown to me he was having the same experience about me. At the end of the programme, he turned to me to introduce himself. We connected so quickly that people who met us that evening assumed that we came to the conference together. At the end of the four-day conference, he was to travel back to his state. Before he left, he shared what he felt about me and how it was unusual for him, since we have not met before. He told me he was praying to God for a life partner, and that from the way he felt, he wanted me to pray about it. Immediately, I told him not to be certain based on his feelings, as I felt the same way too. But I have come to understand that we are in a season where God is aligning His children for His purpose. We must put ourselves aside and let God reign in our affairs. He agreed with me. We kept in touch after the conference, and we attended other conferences together after that one; our feelings towards each other did not change, but because we left it to God and focused on God's kingdom, our friendship blossomed in true agape love. As we both prayed individually, God revealed to us that the purpose of our meeting is not for marriage but for His kingdom. We have a similar calling and have in so many ways encouraged each other in our various places of call. I remember when he came for my book launch some time ago; my friends were shocked to see how we related.

If our affection and love are for God and His kingdom, every other thing will seem secondary and subject to the higher purpose. Amen. I think we have been too silent on these practical issues that challenge our youths daily, trapping them in secret sins and most of the time, heartbreak, as they do not know the right way to approach such friendship.

God is calling His sons and daughters to maturity in Him; the earnest expectation of creation is groaning for the manifestation of the sons of God. We cannot do it alone or achieve it in gender discrimination, like people of the world. We have His power in us; we have been delivered from sin and the power of sin. Alleluia! We are clothed in His righteousness, and His grace abides in us to teach and train us to walk in His righteousness in producing the fruits of holiness. This is our heritage, and it makes us different from the children of the world; the Spirit life enables us to relate as brethren in the fear of the Lord without violating one another and the law of the Lord.

Homosexuality/Lesbianism

Sexual perversion and homosexuality is a great challenge in the twenty-first century, a situation where men and women claim to have deep sexual need for one another in contradiction to God's original purpose. It is even legalised in some countries. God is seated on His throne; His heart hurts because of our perversions, despite His unfailing love for humanity.

Real love is the love shown in God's way; anything done contrary to the will of God is not of God; it's demonic and dehumanizing. It is also absurd to hear people talk of human rights in support of lesbianism and gay relationships.

The Bible says in Romans 1:21-28:

"Because, although they knew God, they did not glorify Him as God, nor were thankful, but became futile in their thoughts, and their foolish hearts were darkened. Professing to be wise, they became fools, and changed the glory of the incorruptible God into an image made like corruptible man – and birds and four-footed animals and creeping things. Therefore, God also gave them up to uncleanness, in the lusts of their hearts, to dishonour their bodies among themselves, who exchanged the truth of God for the lie, and worshiped and served the creature rather than the Creator, who is blessed forever. Amen. For this reason God gave them up to vile passions. For even their women exchanged the natural use for what is against nature. Likewise also the men, leaving the natural use of the woman, burned in their lust for one another, men with men, committing what is shameful, and receiving in themselves the penalty of their error which was due. And even as they did not like to retain God in their knowledge, God gave them over to a debased mind, to do those things which are not fitting."

It is amazing that so many books have been written to encourage teenagers and young adolescents into such acts while some books have been written to soothe themselves that the Bible does not clearly say much about sexual perversions. How on earth could anyone say such things about an all-knowing God who destroyed Sodom and Gomorrah for the same sin? How can they say that of a holy God whose eyes cannot behold iniquity? Truth must be told in love, but "love without truth," Warren Weirsbe said, "is hypocrisy." As we maintain our position of love and a nonjudgmental attitude, we must represent God in His truth.

Please do not allow anyone to deceive you into eternal doom. In the beginning, God created man and woman for procreation and dominion. Satan loves to pervert the things of God because he is a rebel. He, the devil, knows that he has been judged and reserved for hellfire, and he is determined to bring many sons and daughters of God along with him. But Jesus is calling you into glory and eternity with Him in heaven.

In Genesis 1:27-28, we read: *"So God created man in His own image; in the image of God He created him; male and female He created them. Then God blessed them, and God said to them, "Be fruitful and multiply; fill the earth and subdue it; have dominion over the fish of the sea, over the birds of the air, and over every living thing that moves on the earth."* More so, we read the words of Adam in Genesis 2:23 after God presented Eve to Adam, he said *"This is now bone of my bones and flesh of my flesh; She shall be called Woman, because she was taken out of Man."* And the Bible concludes from verses 24 and 25: *"Therefore a man shall leave his father and mother and be joined to his wife, and they shall become one flesh. And they were both naked, the man and his wife, and were not ashamed."* This is God's ordained relationship for marriage; man was formed from the ground and the woman from the rib of the man.

The Bible makes us to understand the efforts God made to make a helper for Adam in Genesis 2:18-20, *"And the LORD God said, 'It is not good that man should be alone; I will make him a helper comparable to him.' Out of the ground the LORD God formed every beast of the field and every bird of the air, and brought them to Adam to see what he would call them. And whatever Adam called each living creature, that was its name. So Adam gave names to all cattle, to the birds of the air, and to every beast of the field. But for Adam there was not found a helper comparable to him."* God presented all the animals formed from the ground to Adam; he saw them and could only name them, and none could serve as a helper comparable to him until the woman was formed from him by God.

Sexual perversions, such as bestiality and homosexuality,

are abominations and a great sign of rebellion to the word of God. If you are reading this book and you are a lesbian, a gay man, a lady who is involved in anal sex for money or fun, or a person who has sexual involvement with animals, hear this: God loves you, but hates what you are doing. I want you to know that Satan orchestrated you into such things because he wants you out of God's plan. He knows that God will not be pleased with you. More so, the devil wants to shorten your lifespan and bring upon you all manner of psychological and health problems, such as anal incontinence, HIV/AIDS, and other sexually transmitted diseases—and to spend eternity with him in hellfire.

Some of you are already suffering from all these ailments, but the love of God is able to heal and make you whole again. If you accept the love of God today, He will change your life. I don't know what led you into it, but God's love is powerful enough to bring you to Himself. God is always willing and ready to forgive and love you as His beloved child. If you are ready to give your heart to the love of God in order to experience the newness of life, please say this prayer aloud:

Lord Jesus, I come to you today as a sinner; have mercy on me. Forgive my sins and iniquity. I denounce Satan and his activities to follow You as My Lord and saviour. I believe in my heart and confess with my mouth that you died and rose on the third day. Wash me with your blood. Thank you for saving me.

Chapter Seven

Saving the World with God's Love

John 3:16 *says, "For God so loved the world that He gave His only begotten Son, that whoever believes in Him should not perish but have everlasting life."*

God's love towards humankind made Him send forth His only Son to save the world and restore His kingdom to the earth. The Bible records in 2 Corinthians 5:19-20: *"[T]hat is, that God was in Christ reconciling the world to Himself, not imputing their trespasses to them, and has committed to us the word of reconciliation. Now then, we are ambassadors for Christ, as though God were pleading through us: we implore you on Christ's behalf, be reconciled to God."*

If God was in Christ reconciling the world—including you and me—to Himself, and has in turn given us the ministry of reconciliation; that is, reconciling others to God through our words and works of love in reaching out to lost souls with the message of salvation and the kingdom of God, then we have no choice but to be obedient to God's commission. The state of our hearts doesn't matter right now; neither does how unloving we think we are or the people of the world are. If we allow the love of God to fill our hearts and surrender our hearts and many shortfalls to God, He will be able to help us develop enough passion for lost souls. The Bible tells us in Daniel 12:3: *"Those who are wise shall shine like the brightness of the firmament. And those who turn many to righteousness like the stars forever."*

More so, we are made to understand in Acts 15:16-18 how God intends to achieve this agenda in these last days. I sincerely believe that our understanding of this will help us greatly in carrying out our mandate of reconciliation of people, cities, and nations to God. The passage states, *"After this I will return and will rebuild the tabernacle of David, which has fallen down; I will rebuild its ruins, and I will set it up; So that the rest of mankind may seek the L<small>ORD</small>, even all the Gentiles who are called by My name, says the L<small>ORD</small> who does all these things. Known to God from eternity are all His works."*

What Is the Tabernacle of David All About?

The Bible makes us understand that we are God's house. His tabernacle is where, with the Lord, we will dwell. This is why Jesus said in John 14:23: *"If anyone loves Me, he will keep My word; and My Father will love him, and We will come to him and make Our home with him."* We read earlier that our love for the Lord spurs us to obedience. In this passage, Jesus says that if we love Him and keep His word, He and the Father will come and make their abode in us. We will become the Lord's tabernacle, His home, and His dwelling place. Alleluia!

David, as the Lord Himself testified of him, was a man after God's heart. He loved the Lord and lived all his life adoring the Lord. This never ruled out his weaknesses and shortfalls, but his reverence for God made him zealous for God—and God's people. As we read in the preface, it was David who affirms that he who must rule people must do so in the fear of the Lord. This same David wrote in the book of Psalms that he has seen the consummation of all perfection.

David was not just a king; he was a lover and a friend of God; this relationship made him one with the Lord. David was the only King in Israel who broke the protocol of the Levitical priesthood because of his love for God. I sincerely believe that just as he wrote in the book of Psalms that his heart pants after the Lord as the deer pants after brooks of water (Psalm 42:1), he could no longer bear to have contact with the Ark of the Covenant once in a year, as the custom was. He had to do something radically different by bringing the Ark of the Covenant—which represented the presence, glory, and power of God—from the house of Obed-Edom to his throne in Jerusalem (see 1 Chronicles). He was an undignified and unrestricted worshipper of God who did not delight in the praise and honour of men even as a king; rather, he was focused on the Lover of his soul. David built a tabernacle for the Ark of the Covenant in Jerusalem. This was plundered and destroyed during Israel's captivity, but the Lord said in the scripture above that He would rebuild the Tabernacle of David that has fallen down and rebuild its ruins so that the rest of humankind would seek the Lord. Amen. I love the way Charles P. Schmitt puts it in his book, *End-Time Truths for End-Time People*, he said, "The tabernacle of David is a study in holy, priestly, anointed simplicity—the adoration of a man deeply in love with His God!"

I sincerely believe that the restoration the Lord is talking about is that of David's pattern of relationship with Him that enabled him to serve him acceptably and rule his people in the fear of the Lord. The Lord will once again enjoy an unbroken relationship with us His people so that we can carry His presence from our personal and corporate altars (the church) to our various place of assignment: to the streets, to the beer parlours, brothels, and our individual thrones where He has apportioned for us to reign. From our relationship with the Lord, we are able to know His will and His mode of operation. Then, we are able to replicate it in our places of assignment—thereby bringing heaven down to the earth. This is the relationship between our priesthood and kingship as God's Royal Priesthood. If our priesthood is not intact, we cannot reign; we cannot reconcile humankind and nations to God.

Until we take our stand as God's priests and kings according to the order of Melchizedek, we will not be able to bring heaven's pattern down to the earth. When we operate as we are called and presented to our God by our Lord Jesus Christ as priests and kings, we become incorruptible and able to walk in dominion in all spheres of life. As the people of the world see the glory of God upon us—His nature of righteousness and justice depicted in all we do—people will want to know more about our God and begin to flock to the house of the Lord. According to Isaiah 2:1-3: *"The word that Isaiah the son of Amoz saw concerning Judah and Jerusalem. Now it shall come to pass in the latter days that the mountain of the LORD's house shall be established on the top of the mountains, and shall be exalted above the hills; and all nations shall flow to it. Many people shall come and say, 'Come, and let us go up to the mountain of the LORD, to the house of the God of Jacob; He will teach us His ways, and we shall walk in His paths.' For out of Zion shall go forth the law and the word of the LORD from Jerusalem."*

How Do We Go About It?

1. *Making Our Priesthood a Reality*

A. Ministering to the Lord and Interceding for All

As God's priests, we must have a deep relationship with the Lord, His word, and His purpose. It is our Spiritual position that makes our physical reign on earth possible because it is through divine relationship that we can be righteous rulers over the earth. We have the obligation of ministering to the Lord and standing before Him on behalf of our family, community, His church, our nation, and the lost amongst us. We are to be God's eyes as His watchmen and intercessors; this is a call of responsibility to all believers, but many of us are too engrossed with our personal needs and desires that we feel this is an assignment for a few brothers and sisters. We are all priests of God and should learn to bear the burden of God's people and all that pertains to His kingdom. This we can only achieve in the place of prayer. It takes love to go to the place of prayer and be selfless; many of us are in the faith so occupied with having personal breakthroughs that we forget that Jesus said we should seek the kingdom of God first and every other thing shall be added unto us (Matthew 6:33).

Love for God and His kingdom makes us stand in the gap for the unsaved souls in our homes and society. To reconcile men, women, cities, and nations to God, we need the love of God in our hearts. As we pray on our knees to God for a change of heart for them, we should be physically and emotionally available to be all we should be in words and deeds for the unsaved by ministering to their needs in practical ways.

As children of God, our minds must be radically changed and attuned to God to be all we are created to be. The Bible says, *"Blessed are those who mourn, for they shall be comforted"* (Matthew 5:4). When we mourn over our unsaved families, friends, loved ones, and nation, God will comfort us by opening their hearts—like Lydia in the Bible (Acts 16:14-15)—to heed the gospel. This is our place as people of God. In the words of Andrew Murray, in his book The Secret of Intercession, he said: "There is nothing that can bring us nearer to God and lead us deeper into His love than the work of intercession. Nothing can give us a higher experience of the likeness of God than the power of pouring out our hearts into the bosom of God in prayer for people around us."

We must develop the attitude of praying for God's church irrespective of the denomination we belong to; we pray that the church become triumphant and the saints become more like Jesus till His return.

It is only through prayer that we can deliver the hearts of humankind from the hand of the enemy. The Bible says the God of this world has blinded them so that they will not see the light of the gospel of Christ (John 12:40; 2 Corinthians 4:4). We have to pray that their eyes be opened; we have to pull down every stronghold of the enemy in their minds — each exalting itself above the knowledge of the word of God. I remember one of the days when the Nigerian Islamic sect Boko Haram burnt two churches in different locations in one Sunday, I felt so bad and bitter that I began to pray dangerous prayers like I have never prayed before. The Holy Spirit interrupted me and said, "Oh Mother in Israel, these prayers will not help us to profit in this!" He referred me to 2 Corinthians 10:4-6, *"For the weapons of our warfare are not carnal but mighty in God for pulling down strongholds, casting down arguments and every high thing that exalts itself against the knowledge of God, bringing every thought into captivity to the obedience of Christ, and being ready to punish all disobedience when your obedience is fulfilled."* I immediately changed my prayer point to pulling down strongholds and the powers behind them. As I did this, I had peace that at the end of the difficult period of persecution of the church that the Lord God will be gracious to us; that we will profit in it. I believe that most of those persecuting the church — as Paul the apostle once did—will be convicted by the Most High. Many of these men will be saved from Satan's hold on their lives, while our nation will be regained to the Lord in Jesus's name. Amen.

There is no seed sown that has no reward from God. We need to pray that our eyes of understanding be enlightened by God to be able to see beyond our individual vision. We need to see His kingdom built and be able to help any growing ministry or person on a divine assignment in whatever capacity we can—especially in interceding for them.

I love the way Paul E. Billheimer puts it in his book, *Destined for the Throne*. He said, "If the church does not pray God will not act, because that would nullify His plan to prepare her for rulership through on-the job training in enforcing Christ's victory at Calvary." Prayer, he said, "is God's appointed means of accomplishing His work in the world."

B. Evangelising the Truth in Love

Our key assignment is to preach the heavenly kingdom to those who have yet to know the Lord. If we do not have deep love in our hearts for God, it becomes a burden reaching out to lost souls because there will be no passion driving us to follow such a noble course. We might become weary along the way. When we try to minister to the lost, we might not be able to touch their hearts; instead, we reach their minds. As we say things that appeal to them to come with us to our church, but still are not convicting enough for them to turn over their lives to God from their sinful state, we can get frustrated.

I remember when we started the church mass evangelism on fixed days—mostly Saturdays. I discovered that some people were not ready to give attention to the gospel; let alone listen to what we had to say. Because of this, at times we just gave out tracts or gave hopeful messages of: "If you come to Jesus, your sickness will be healed; poverty will turn to prosperity" and similar statements. Those words were consoling and true in Christ, but that is not the gospel. Yes, we have been able to bring quite a number of people to church this way, but how many of these people have truly stayed in the kingdom or even understood the kingdom of God outside their relationship of seeking solutions to their immediate needs from God?

We are to preach that the kingdom of God has come, but no person can see and enter it without absolute repentance of old ways. It is love that gives such audacity to point a man or woman to an aspect of his or her life that he or she is afraid to look at. To let them know that such sinful lifestyles do not conform to the kingdom and destroy destiny, to give them reasons—with proof from our own lives—why they should do away with such lifestyles. It is our personal encounters with God and the fire in our hearts for His kingdom and humanity that encourage and give us the boldness to say what needs to be said in love, without being judgmental. But how could we ever do this if our priesthood is questionable or not activated? Until our prayer altars are on fire and we have won the battle for the souls of these people on our knees, forces out there will be stronger than the Word we speak to them—if our words are not filled with power from God's presence.

I sincerely believe that every one of us has a history with the Lord; of where He picked us from and changed our lives. I have a friend who used to be in the occult before he gave his life to Christ. Because of all the battles God fought for him when his fellow cult members came after him, he saw the power of God on display in saving and changing his life. According to him, his reason for joining the occult was for protection; this, he discovered, was mere deceit. Only God can save and preserve. Any time he goes out to evangelise, his testimony and encounter with God gives him the conviction that the gospel he is preaching is not fake but authentic; the spirit and power behind the testimony, which is the Spirit of God, empowers his words convicting the souls.

I remember a particular day when I just felt reluctant going for the mass evangelism because I saw people whose personal lives showed that they themselves didn't understand the gospel they preach or even the God they were speaking to people about. At the end of the day, people are brought into the church with expectations of coming to meet the God Who will solve all their problems — not understanding the depth of His love, what He did on the cross, and how much it cost Him to save them.

As I pondered about this, the Spirit began to minister to me that the reason why there are so many immature and powerless Christians is because of the kind of gospel that brought them to church in the first place. When many of them don't get solutions to their problems immediately, they are quick to complain, quit coming to church, or keep jumping from one church to another. At that point, I made up my mind that no matter how the people behave, I will be bold in my approach to preaching the gospel and say what I have to say in love. I make sure I pray before I leave for evangelism. On two different occasions, I found myself on the outskirts of Abuja City in Nigeria, an area inhabited by prostitutes.

As I stepped into one of the restaurants, I saw young ladies dressed half naked. Their faces suddenly became unfriendly, especially when they saw me with my Bible, but I was not discouraged. I took a seat next to one of them; I had books with me that I normally give out for free during evangelism. I smiled at them and ignored their unfriendly looks. Suddenly I began to speak to them about the love of God, how much He loves them, and desires changes in their lives—if they believe that all their sins have been taken care of at the cross. I began to demonstrate what happens at the cross; Satan has been defeated and has no power or right over their lives.

I told them that Satan is aware of God's love for them and wants them to think that God doesn't care; I made them understand that God hates to see men abuse them for peanuts. My eyes were filled with tears, and suddenly they all got weak. I implored them to ponder what I had told them about God's love when they get to their homes. They were so convicted that one of them said, "Aunty, I don't like what I am doing, but if I stop now, how will I survive?" I told her that if she would just believe and speak to God as a Father, He would make a way for her. I ministered to and prayed along with them.

As Christians and beloved of God, love should send us to the streets ministering to people the truth of God's word. That will convict men and women of their real state with God so that they could be convinced enough to respond to God's love from their hearts. Men and women must not come to God on the foundation of what He will do for them; there is nothing wrong in expecting solutions to one's problems from God—but we must first make men and women respond to His love by appreciating Him for what He did on the cross to save them. This appreciation will make them want to know who He really is. Any person who comes to Jesus on this foundation of deep conviction and love always survives against all odds, yet remains in the faith. From the scriptures, we saw that Jesus Himself spoke in love to people about the truth of the kingdom. He told them that it would cost them their lives to follow Him. He told them a parable of counting one's cost before thinking of building a tower (Luke 14:28). In this end time, it is our obligation to bring people to Christ with the intent that eternity does not elude them. We are in the era when our salvation is closer than when we first believed. The enemy is raging and inventing all manner of evil to take people away from God; we cannot compete with the enemy with strategies that are synonymous with his. It is only when we speak the right scriptural words to people—as Jesus did—that the Holy Spirit can convict people because He works with *His* words, not our words.

2. *Operating in the consciousness of our Kingship*

I believe that if we are conscious of the fact that we have been presented to our God by our Lord Jesus Christ as kings, we will comport ourselves accordingly here on earth and live radically different lives for all to see. There is a place and an assignment God has apportioned for every one of us. There is a place of call, a city, and a nation that He has allotted to us to reign over. If we do not align ourselves with this kingdom purpose, our lives will be frustrated—no matter how churchy we are. Living out the consciousness of our kingship enables us to see not just beyond the church or God's people, but God's intention for His entire creation—including unsaved nations and people. Until we broaden our perspective, we will continually put God in a box. God is the King of the universe and the desire of all nations, yet many of these nations have yet to hear about Him or accept Him as their Lord and saviour. This is why He sent us as heaven's ambassadors to come and show the people of the earth the heavenly lifestyle and give them hope of being members of the kingdom.

Every kingdom has its principles of operation, just as the kingdom of God does. We have the word of God to guide us. Through His word, we know that the foundation of God was built on righteousness and justice; this should also be our foundation as God's people sent to replicate heaven's pattern of doing things here on earth.

Jesus, in Matthew 5:3-12, taught His disciples what the attitude of heaven's citizens should be: *"Blessed are the poor in spirit, for theirs is the kingdom of heaven. Blessed are those who mourn, for they shall be comforted. Blessed are the meek, for they shall inherit the earth. Blessed are those who hunger and thirst for righteousness, for they shall be filled. Blessed are the merciful, for they shall obtain mercy. Blessed are the pure in heart, for they shall see God. Blessed are the peacemakers, for they shall be called sons of God. Blessed are those who are persecuted for righteousness' sake, for theirs is the kingdom of heaven. Blessed are you when they revile and persecute you, and say all kinds of evil against you falsely for My sake. Rejoice and be exceedingly glad, for great is your reward in heaven, for so they persecuted the prophets who were before you."*

We see from the above scriptures that there are attitudes as God's ambassadors that we need to absorb that will differentiate us from those in the world, these beatitudes taught by our Lord Jesus Christ are irresistible traits. As God's own people, we must hunger for righteousness. We must be merciful to others. Our hearts must be pure because out of them come the issues of life. If our hearts are not pure, we cannot see God. The truth is that only those with pure hearts can ascend the holy hills of God, according to Psalm 24:3-4. We should be poor in spirit, depending on the Lord absolutely always; we must be meek, willing to be taught and to be led by the Lord. We must mourn in order to be comforted by the Lord. We are to be peacemakers—rejoicing always, no matter what the persecution or what we experience because we have our reward in heaven. Our minds should be heavenly focused because that is where we belong. How then, do we bring these to bear as we relate with one another in the kingdom and as we reach out to those outside the kingdom with the intent of reconciling them with God?

A. *Dress and Behave Like Royalty*

Our lifestyles and modes of dressing must not betray our citizenship as kings and queens; we must reflect who we are in our behaviour and clothing. People should see us and without being told, know that we are from another kingdom and not of this world. I get so worried about the way we have adopted other people's cultures as kingdom culture, especially in our modes of dressing. In God's kingdom, there are principles and order; holiness is the highway of God. As His people, we must not compromise this. If we are going to be bold in preaching the kingdom and manifesting heaven's pattern, we must not throw our modesty and decency into the dustbin. We are to be gentle people, not quarrelsome or given to drunkenness. We are to hate iniquity and love righteousness and justice. If we adhere to and obey God's commandments, it will reflect in our outward appearance. Remember, we are the "fragrance of Christ," according to the scriptures (2 Corinthians 2:15), which means that everywhere we go—before we open our mouths to mention Christ—from our appearance and conduct, people should know that we belong to Him.

B. *Walking and Working in Unity of Purpose*

Whether we believe it or not, people are watching us; especially the unbelievers or Christians who are weak in faith and still struggling to have enough reason to be committed to God.

In John 13:34-35, Jesus told His disciples that, *"A new commandment I give to you, that you love one another; as I have loved you, that you also love one another. By this all will know that you are My disciples, if you have love for one another."* From this scripture we understand that it is the love we have for one another as believers that will make the world know that we are His disciples. People of the world are groping in darkness—feeling much hatred, envy, and strife; yet, they desire peace and quietness and do not know how to get it. If these people see the way we live our lives as believers and God's own ambassadors and kings, relating with one another in love irrespective of our denominations, our conduct of love will minister to them. But when Christians war against Christians or backbite about one another, we make the Gentiles profane the name of our God. This makes the kingdom of God unattractive to them.

One of the prayers of Jesus before he departed from the earth is found in John 17:21: *"That they all may be one, as You, Father are in Me, and I in You; that they also may be one in Us, that the world may believe that you sent Me."* Those are the words of our saviour. The Bible says there is only one foundation on which we are built; it is the foundation of Christ—not any person. So many Christians are getting it all twisted as we "play church" and tend to speak unkindly of other brethren who do not belong to our denomination or church; it is unscriptural and should not be encouraged among believers.

We are all Christ's—and should relate in brotherly and sisterly love. Sometimes I wonder why it is so difficult to obey the injunction of the scriptures; Jesus said a kingdom divided against itself cannot stand (Matthew 12:25). It is the people in the evil world that believe this wisdom more than the Christians. Witches, wizards, the occult, and New Age people are always quick to relate in brotherly and sisterly love above their own natural families. This is why their kingdom appears to be creating all manner of havoc to us in the kingdom of God.

If we relate in unity of purpose, there will be more demonstrations of the power of God in our churches, individual lives, and nations. I sincerely believe that there are so many things we have to repent from and ask for mercy; because even at our pulpits, there are statements and words we say that grieve the Holy Spirit or even make a sinner coming to church for the first time not to give his or her life to God. We must stop making derogatory statements about denominations that are different from ours, no matter what. Jesus desires unity in His church so that He can move by His Spirit mightily, putting the house of the Lord on top of the mountain that will make the Gentiles flow into the kingdom. 1 Corinthians 12:25 says, *"[T]hat there should be no schism in the body, but that the members should have the same care for one another."* Love helps us to see the brotherly and sisterly relationship as members of God's family the way it really is. We must begin to speak about God and His kingdom and not denominations. The Bible says in Jeremiah 9:23-24: *"Thus says the Lord: 'let not the wise man glory in his wisdom, let not the mighty man glory in his might, nor let the rich man glory in his riches. But let him who glories glory in this, that he understands and knows Me, that I am the Lord, exercising lovingkindness, judgment, and righteousness in the earth. For in these I delight,' says the Lord."* This should be our ultimate boast and declaration to the world around us.

There is a popular song we sing as a body of Christ. Part of it goes like this, "We are joint heirs with the Son, we are children of the kingdom, we are family, and we are one." If we truly believe the words in this song, we will relate with one another differently. But we sing it because it makes us feel good; yet, we are not connected.

I believe that church leadership has a large role to play in bringing about unity amongst believers. Jesus did not come to preach about denominations; thus, we must disconnect ourselves from this. Whether we like it or not, Jesus is not coming for a denomination but a glorious, united church in spirit. If heaven is our focus, we must begin to relate as God has called us to. In Ephesians 4:11-13 (AMP) the Bible says, *"And [His gifts to the church were varied and] He Himself appointed some as apostles [special messengers, representatives], some as prophets [who speak a new message from God to the people], some as evangelists [who spread the good news of salvation], and some as pastors and teachers [to shepherd and guide and instruct], [and He did this] to fully equip and perfect the saints (God's people) for works of service, to build up the body of Christ [the church]; until we all reach oneness in the faith and in the knowledge of the Son of God, [growing spiritually] to become a mature believer, reaching to the measure of the fullness of Christ [manifesting His spiritual completeness and exercising our spiritual gifts in unity]."*

The essence of our difference in ministry is to equip the saints into maturity with the intent that we attain oneness in the faith and in the comprehension of the knowledge of the Son of God. Saints should be properly furnished to mature to the point of no bias or discrimination against one another regarding denominations. The truth is that when the enemy attacks, he doesn't care whether the assembly is Catholic, Anglican, or Pentecostal; all the enemy knows is that Jesus is preached in that assembly. May God give us understanding in Jesus's name. Amen. This is why the Bible tells us in Philippians 1:27-28 (AMP):

"Only [be sure to] lead your lives in a manner [that will be] worthy of the gospel of Christ, so that whether I do come and see you or remain absent, I will hear about you that you are standing firm in one spirit [and one purpose], with one mind striving side by side [as if in combat] for the faith of the gospel. And in no way be alarmed or intimidated [in anything] by your opponents, for such [constancy and fearlessness on your part] is a [clear] sign [a proof and a seal] for them of [their impending] destruction, but [a clear sign] for you of deliverance and salvation, and that too, from God."

Our unity will not only make us experience the power of God to bring about revival; it will also expose the destructive end of the enemies of the church. Alleluia!

C. *A Life of Generosity*

Kings are generous people and use their resources for their kingdom and subjects. It is impossible for us to attempt to reach out to souls for God without giving of our time, resources, love, and kindness. We read in the first chapter of this book that love gives. The Bible says in Zechariah 1:17: *"Again proclaim, saying 'thus says the* Lord *of hosts: 'my cities shall again spread out through prosperity; the* Lord *will again comfort Zion, and will again choose Jerusalem.'"* As children of His love, His course must be our course. We must reach out with all that we have to bring souls into His kingdom; there is nothing we have that is ours. John the Baptist said no man receives anything except if it is given from above (John 3:27).

God has blessed us to be a blessing. There are so many young people today on the streets and even in churches who, out of frustration, have found themselves involved in unrighteous acts to survive, pay school fees, and to eat. Yet we come to the house of God to show off our cars and latest clothes to others. There is nothing wrong with having flashy things, but there is everything wrong when God has blessed us, and we are not thinking about helping other people to forge ahead righteously.

Whatever God has blessed us with is given to us to expand His kingdom. Let us begin to look around us, to enquire about areas of need among people in our local assemblies, on the streets, and in corners where people dare not go. Our light is to shine in darkness. If we go to brothels, we will save many ladies and young men from prostitution; we will give their lives meaning by bringing them to the saving knowledge of Jesus.

Evangelism is beyond talking to people about the gospel or sharing tracts; we must demonstrate the compassion Jesus demonstrated while He walked on earth. He preached the kingdom, fed the hungry, and healed the sick.

I remember during one of our Saturday evangelism meetings in Kaduna state. We went to one of the hideouts in the Narayi area, where young men gather to drink heavily and smoke Indian hemp. Initially, they all looked scary with their unkempt hair, dirty environment, and so on. I went in with my partner and we began to speak to them. There was this particular guy who had all manner of rings—each a different shape—on his fingers. He looked rugged and tough. He stood by the corner and watched us preach to others, he motioned towards me and said: "Aunty, tell me wetin you dey tell them." I was touched, so I turned to minister to him. As I began, I noticed a change in his countenance and a willingness to accept Christ. I led him to Jesus. The Spirit ministered to me that the guy was hungry, but I was battling with myself. While I was trying to sort myself out, he told me that he would love to go to church, but he did not have the means; and he had not eaten. Immediately, I gave him some money to buy food and go to church. He looked at me with tears in his eyes. This man confessed to me; he wanted his life to be better, but he did not know how to begin. I left him with a heavy heart and prayed to God for resources to save souls like this young man.

I told my partner that if I had my way right there, I would ensure that all the people we ministered to get a shower and shave, received clothes to wear and underwent rehabilitation for a better quality of life. That is what Jesus would do. He did it for the man possessed by demons that he healed in Luke 8:35: *"Then they went out to see what had happened, and came to Jesus, and found the man from whom the demons had departed, sitting at the feet of Jesus, clothed and in his right mind. And they were afraid."* Jesus the King of kings gave His all to the point of death; why is it difficult for us?

It is time we lay our treasures at God's altar and begin to fight His course. This is real faith and real love, my brothers and sisters. Life spent giving is a life that you are actually living. Jesus said that where your treasure is, there your heart will be (Matthew 6:21; Luke 12:34). If our treasure is in heaven, our hearts will be fixed on heaven while we reign on earth.

The teaching of Jesus on His return in judgment in Matthew 25:31–45 is a must-read; please read with me: *"When the Son of Man comes in His glory, and all the holy angels with Him, then He will sit on the throne of His glory. All the nations will be gathered before Him, and He will separate them one from another, as a shepherd divides his sheep from the goats. And He will set the sheep on His right hand, but the goats on the left.*

"Then the King will say to those on His right hand 'come, you blessed of My Father, inherit the kingdom prepared for you from the foundation of the world: 'for I was hungry and you gave Me food; I was thirsty and you gave Me drink; I was a stranger and you took Me in; 'I was naked and you clothed Me; I was sick and

you visited Me; I was in prison and you came to Me' "*then the righteous will answer him, saying, 'Lord, when did we see You hungry and feed You, or thirsty and give You drink? 'When did we see You a stranger and take You in, or naked and clothe You? Or when did we see You sick, or in prison and come to You?'* "*and the King will answer and say to them, 'Assuredly, I say to you, inasmuch as you did it to one of the least of these My brethren, you did it to Me.'*

"*Then He will also say to those on the left hand, 'depart from Me, you cursed, into the everlasting fire prepared for the devil and his angels: 'for I was hungry and you gave Me no food; I was thirsty and you gave Me no drink; I was a stranger and you did not take Me in, naked and you did not clothe Me, sick and in prison and you did not visit Me.' Then they also will answer Him, saying, 'Lord, when did we see You hungry or thirsty or a stranger or naked or sick or in prison, and did not minister to You?'* "*Then He will answer them saying, 'assuredly, I say to you, inasmuch as you did not do it to one of the least of these, you did not do it to Me.'*"

As I wrote earlier, all human beings are important to God because we are created in His image; divinity exists in everyone, and we must heed what the Spirit of the Lord is saying.

Chapter Eight

End Time Warning: Our Love Must Not Go Cold!

It is worthy to note that the scriptures warned us of the nature of our hearts as we approach the end of time. When the disciples of Jesus Christ asked Him about the sign of His coming and the end of the age, the Bible records in Matthew 24:4-14: *And Jesus answered and said to them, "Take heed that no one deceives you. For many will come in My name, saying, 'I am Christ,' and will deceive many. And you will hear of wars and rumours of wars. See that you are not troubled, for all these things must come to pass, but the end is not yet. For nation will rise against nation, and kingdom against kingdom. And there will be famine, pestilences, and earthquakes in various places. All these are the beginning of sorrows. Then, they will deliver you to tribulation and kill you, and you will be hated by all nations for My name's sake. And then, many will be offended, will betray one another, and will hate one another. Then many false prophets will rise up and deceive many. And because lawlessness will abound, the love of many will go cold. But he who endures to the end shall be saved. And this gospel of the kingdom will be preached in the entire world as a witness to all the nations, and then the end will come."*

From these scriptures, we see Jesus warning us of the dangers ahead; which indeed is the season we are in now. If we look around the world today, there is much suspicion about who a genuine person of God is and who is not, because men and women have grown to become lovers of themselves, greed, and money; calling themselves into ministry when God did not call them, and causing confusion everywhere. This has made a lot of Christians lose faith in going to church. They would prefer to stay in their homes because they are sick of what is happening in the church. About five years ago, I boarded a bus from Abuja to Port Harcourt to attend a prayer conference organised by Intercessors for Nigeria. On the way, the bus driver was very engrossed in the gospel music he was playing, and that prompted me to start a discussion with him. Then we began to talk about the church in Nigeria. To my surprise, he told me that he doesn't go to church because he is sceptical of who is really called of God. Even though he is not the first person who has said that to me, it touched me because he said it with so much bitterness and anger. The truth is that no matter what we feel about people of God, we must respect the fact that they said they are called of God. If your spirit does not agree to fellowship in a particular place, pray to God to lead you to a place where you can fellowship with Him in spirit and in truth because the Bible enjoins us not to forsake the assembly of the brethren. Another thing we should learn from Jesus Christ is this: when His disciples told Him about those preaching the gospel which they felt were not of Christ, Jesus told His disciples that for as long as they are preaching the gospel in His name, it doesn't matter. This shows that they are for Him and not against Him; but in a situation where it is proven, and we are convinced that their mode of operation is dependent on another power outside God that could lead those following them to hellfire, we can prayerfully ask God to expose them and deliver their followers. We also read through the mind of Paul the apostle when he said it doesn't matter to him whether anyone preaches Christ in truth or deceit for selfish gains; but what matters is that Christ is being preached. We are not in the position to judge anyone because God knows those whom He called, and Jesus already told us that there are those who will come to Him on Judgment Day—that they have cast out demons in His name. But He will tell them that He does not know them because they are workers of iniquity. Only Jesus has the authority to say that to anyone—not us; our role is to ensure that the Spirit of God is active in our lives, guiding and leading us on the path that leads Godward.

More so, each day we watch on our television screens events happening all over the world: the dead bodies of innocent lives from suicide bombings, religious crises, war and economic crises, and so on. In Nigeria, we have the challenge of Boko Haram, the Islamic sect warring against Western education in their region by killing the innocent. They have created a lot of fear and tension amongst tribes and religious sects, and distrust between the government and the people. People are getting angrier, more aggressive, and more hostile by the day. Bitterness and hatred are consciously and unconsciously creeping into our lives. Some people are beginning to doubt the existence of God.

As Christians, our attitudes must be different from others in the face of all these trials. Jesus already told us of the things that will come upon the earth in these last days, which is why we are to abide in Him in obedience to His word, so that nothing can make us afraid: He said we should not be troubled because He has overcome the world for us. Yet, we must not allow our love for God and humankind to grow cold. as Jesus already told us, that because lawlessness will abound, the love of many will grow cold. We have to continuously pray and be on guard so that our salvation will not be stolen from us by the devil, remember, the Bible says, only those that endure to the end shall be saved.

Our salvation in Christ is to be worked on with fear and trembling (2 Corinthians 7:15), according to the apostle Paul's epistle. When we believe and confess Christ, we are saved from sin and the power of sin; He made His grace available to continually help us work out our salvation till the return of Jesus Christ, when we will be taken away from the presence of sin forever. But if we do not watch and pray in this end time, we might turn our faces from His grace that is leading us daily on His path. Instead, we may begin to look towards all that is happening in the world. Like the apostle Peter, who took his face away from Jesus because of the wind when He asked him to walk on the sea, we begin to sink as our faith turns to doubt. May God give us understanding and help us in Jesus's name. Amen.

No matter how bad we feel about situations around us, our hearts must be kept together in God while we pray — hoping in Him for grace to pull through and for the possible changes we want to see. It is only when we keep our hearts steadfast in the love of God that we can endure to the end. 2 Timothy 3:1–4 says, *"But know this, that in the last days perilous times will come: for men will be lovers of themselves, lovers of money, boasters, proud, blasphemers, disobedient to parents, unthankful, unholy, unloving, unforgiving, slanderers, without self control, brutal, despisers of good, traitors, headstrong, haughty, lovers of pleasure rather than lovers of God."*

My prayer is that as we seek to live and walk in the love of God in these last days, we will resist every enemy — such as bitterness, hatred, anger, and everything listed in the above scripture that might get in the way between eternity and us.

I enjoin us to search our hearts to see if there is any wickedness or form of unrighteousness in us that does not glorify God, hindering us from abiding in His love. Let us repent of them all, asking God by His mercy and the help of the Holy Spirit to come into our lives and make us an epitome of His love.

There is so much hope for us if we endure to the end to consummate our marriage with the Lord at the marriage supper of the Lamb. I love to read the book of Revelation because it gives me hope that one day I will no longer need faith to see the invisible God, but I will see Him and be united with Him. I do not know about you, but my desire is that God by His grace will help me to love Him to the end.

When I read through the scriptures I see the challenges of the end time: wars, famines, tribulation, and the hope that in the midst of it all, God has remnants who have been marked as His servants, and that they would be protected and preserved for Him. My earnest prayer remains that my life becomes acceptable to Him.

My prayer is that God helps us individually to secure our hearts and be grounded in His love so that no matter what, our love for Him and creation comes each day anew. Amen.

Jesus Is Coming Soon! Maranatha!

In the early hours of 27 October 2012, I heard the Spirit of the Lord speak to my heart clearly: "Daily prepare for the coming of the soon-coming King."

I have no doubt we are in the times when we are to be driven by eternity in all we do; therefore, this book will be incomplete without a mention of the return of our Lord Jesus Christ.

The essence of God's love is that one day there will be consummation of the church, the Bride of Christ—which we are—and Christ Himself, our heavenly Bridegroom. Sometimes I try to imagine what it will be like, but it's too much for me to comprehend that Almighty God Himself desires an eternal union with me as a member of His church. It is worth looking forward to. This is why I advise that we live our lives driven by love and driven by eternity every day.

The book of Revelation should be a frequent read for every Christian who loves the Lord and desires to see Him someday because it keeps us in perpetual consciousness of the return of Jesus Christ. If we are not conscious of His return in our daily work for and walk with Him, we might go our own way or be lost in the world.

Revelation 22:7 says, *"Behold, I am coming quickly! Blessed is he who keeps the words of the prophecy of this book."* And verses 12–16 state, *"And behold, I am coming quickly, and My reward is with Me, to give to everyone according to his work. I am the Alpha and the Omega, the Beginning and the End, the First and the Last."* *Blessed are those who do His commandments that they may have the right to the tree of life, and may enter through the gates into the city. But outside are dogs and sorcerers and sexually immoral and murderers and idolaters, and whoever loves and practices a lie.* *"I, Jesus, have sent My angel to testify to you these things in the churches. I am the Root and the Offspring of David, the Bright and Morning Star."*

Let us be observant, watch, and pray—and not be like the five foolish virgins that do not have enough oil. Instead, let us be like the five wise virgins who had more than enough oil out of their desperation to meet with their groom. My heart cry is that when Jesus comes, we will be found ready. Amen.

Epilogue

I deeply appreciate God for His unfailing love towards us. He never gives up on us, in spite of our unfaithfulness; yet, He calls us back to Himself through His messengers in various ways. While we reign here on earth, we will be with Him in heaven.

If this book has blessed you, I would appreciate your comments and testimonies. For counselling, please contact me at: info@graceonotu.com, grace.onotu3@gmail.com, and www.graceonotu.com.

Other Books by Dr. Grace Ozioma Onotu

1. *The Future Ones* — Making an impact in the world (2001)

2. *Unravelled Quest* — A peep into the truth of life while growing up (2004)

3. *Real Babes Love Jesus* — Fulfilling your purpose in a perverse generation as a lady on a mission (2012)

4. *Finding Meaning in Difficult Times* — Secrets to exceptional living for a larger-than-life experience (2012) Foreword by Dr Steve Ogan.

Please note that Dr. Grace Ozioma Onotu used to be known as Dr. Zainab Ozioma Onotu before her conversion from the Islamic faith.

www.ingramcontent.com/pod-product-compliance
Lightning Source LLC
Chambersburg PA
CBHW030327080526
44584CB00012B/740